THIS BOOK
BELONGS TO:

_____

LINENS

LINENS

FOR EVERY ROOM AND OCCASION

JANE SCOTT HODGES

FOREWORD BY CHARLOTTE MOSS
PHOTOGRAPHS BY PAUL COSTELLO

RIZZOLI
NEW YORK

New York · Paris · London · Milan

CONTENTS

FOREWORD

CHARLOTTE MOSS

 THE PLEASURES OF LIFE ARE MANY, but there are two that immediately and always come to my mind. First is the joy of entertaining friends at home. The entire planning process is a creative exercise, one that often begins at the end with, What is my table going to look like? How is it going to be set? What linens shall I use? The people, the flowers, the food, my choice of linens . . . for heaven's sake, all must be simpatico for the occasion. Will it be a monogram? Will it be the placemats embroidered with orange tubs? Or maybe the tablecloth from Istanbul with the dyed, antique damask napkins found in France? Whatever the final decision for the evening, you can rest assured that it began with me meditatively staring into the drawers of my linen cabinet, contemplating a scheme. Before I finally settle on a plan for the evening, I will have dreamed up and schemed up innumerable combinations for future luncheons and dinners, and much time will have been spent adding to my "lookout for" shopping list, which lives in my pocketbook.

There is always new territory to explore, some new colored linen to try, a new monogram style, an appliqué, a twisted-thread combination that has always intrigued me. And then, there is that second pleasure. The joy of slipping into beautiful sheets at the end of a long day, perhaps at the end of a successful dinner party, when all the guests have gone home. Crisp linen sheets, intricately embroidered across the edge of the top sheet, the lightest soufflé of a duvet cover, and it's off to never-never land—a rewarding end to a satisfying day. Then when morning comes and another day begins, what better send-off than knowing that same bed will be beckoning you home, home, home again.

But there is another very important and essential part of this equation, for these linens do not just show up in the cupboard! There are people with whom, as an interior decorator, I've built relationships over the years. There are "trade secrets," special resources, and those talented people upon whom I rely for the special things for my clients. Some provide services and wise advice, some provide goods, some provide both, and I can assure you that we could not function or deliver without all of them. Among life's pleasures is being able to collaborate with others who enjoy what they do and are good at it, for their enthusiasm spills over into every one of our joint projects. In fact, sometimes we have to contain the enthusiasm, as we all know how that translates in "ye olde" decorating budget.

I met Jane Scott Hodges when Leontine Linens was a mere infant. Years on, and heaven only knows how many sheets, towels, placemats, cocktail napkins, bathrobes, pj's, travel sets, satin eye covers for sleeping, later . . . what haven't we done? We have had fun, created many gorgeous things for my very happy clients, and laughed ourselves silly through the process. We have traveled together, and when she has been my house-guest, you better believe that I made sure the bed would be suitable for the priestess of pillows and placemats. I have always appreciated and valued her input and guidance on projects. Jane Scott brings Southern savvy and style to the parts of our households and heritage that link us to our grandmothers and daughters alike, and she does it with a great sense of color, a wicked wit, and limitless enthusiasm for what she does . . . well, you, too, will see that in the pages that follow. Jane Scott may know the contents of my linen closets better than I do. She will remember what color thread we used in the aqua guest room in the country, what shade of gray in my bathroom in New York, the linen appliqué on a client's bedcover, and so it goes. Sitting down and putting together an order becomes a laugh fest. The conversation will take off at ninety miles per hour and in as many directions, but eventually, it will settle down to the business at hand. What a pleasure, and that was where we started, right?

The most exciting aspect of anyone's Leontine relationship is the moment of delivery, when UPS arrives. Once the exterior packaging has been ripped apart, the candy shop–colored lavender boxes tied with ribbon of the same color will be visible. Inside, under tissue, are your new treasures, only revealed after slowly peeling back the stickers. With excitement, you remove them from the box as if a new couture evening dress has finally arrived. Then, in a small lavender envelope is a note thanking you for your order and offering suggestions for how to prolong the life of the new additions to your linen chest. How thoughtful, yes, indeed, for now you can enjoy the pleasures of life even longer.

Previous pages, left: Charlotte Moss creates a bed fit for a queen with an unexpected pop of lilac appliqué in an otherwise blue room that is both majestic and serene. Opposite: Charlotte Moss's linen closet in her East Hampton home. Following pages: Handsome twin beds adorned with an appliqué cipher-style monogram in a room by Brian J. McCarthy.

INTRODUCTION

A THING OF BEAUTY IS A JOY FOREVER

A thing of beauty is a joy for ever:
Its loveliness increases; it will never
Pass into nothingness; but still will keep
A bower quiet for us, and a sleep
Full of sweet dreams, and health, and quiet breathing.

—John Keats

I LIKE TO IMAGINE that when John Keats wrote this classic poem, he had just climbed into bed and tucked into his monogrammed linen sheets. Whatever the particular "thing of beauty" he had in mind at the time, his words do seem a perfect way to describe the timeless touch of comfort and luxury that fine linens bring to our lives; they are, indeed, a "joy for ever," and their loveliness increases each time we use them.

Keats hailed from nineteenth-century England, a time and place in which custom linens didn't carry the rather standoffish reputation they've acquired since. They were an assumed aspect of everyday living to those with even modest means, going back centuries. Yet even with their long history as items to be enjoyed and engaged with on a regular basis, modern times have, for too many of us, turned fine linens into anachronisms.

How did we get to the point that we've locked away something so essential to daily pleasure? Maybe custom, hand-worked linens became too associated with grandmothers and dowager aunts, with trunks in attics, their voices too much echoes of the past.

Well, I'm here to tell you that this doesn't have to be the case (or sheet or napkin). We don't live in the past and neither should *what* we live with. Classic values should be embraced, but that doesn't mean you can't infuse them with new ideas.

Every one of us has a distinct voice, and whether classic or modern, quirky or quiet, custom linens are uniquely adaptable to that voice. If you don't speak in lace and eyelet and ivory, why should your bedroom? If your friends refer to you as colorful and unpredictable, they should be referring to your dining room the same way. Yes, there is always

What once was old is new again. What appears to be an antique linen guest towel is actually a contemporary piece, the very definition of a modern-day heirloom.

a place for simple and white, Grandmother dear, but let's start giving due respect to self-expression.

As you tuck into the following pages, you'll see how much fine linens can provide a fresh voice of individuality. I'm not suggesting that people can be folded up into neat chapters, but hopefully you'll see a bit of yourself in some of the great spaces and pieces depicted here—and be inspired. What you'll definitely discover are endless interpretations of appliqué, embroidery, and monograms; myriad weaves and colors to explore; and the places these special items can go, places that you—and your grandmother—never thought of. Remember throughout that bringing personal expression to an aspect of day-to-day life that you may have previously taken for granted is one of the surest ways to stamp your home as unique, as something no one else can copy.

And just so you're not inclined to flip through the pretty pictures once and then stick the book on that high shelf with *The Lost Watercolors of Fra Lippo Lippi*, I've inserted liberal doses of advice on care and use and have called on many trusted friends and advisers to add their wisdom to the proceedings. *Linens: For Every Room and Occasion*, is intended to be equal parts visual inspiration and useful information, to be as engaging and smile-inducing as an armoire full of embroidered bedding and monogrammed Turkish towels . . . or an appliquéd table runner that pulls out the blues in your ancestral tapestry, a pique robe you slip on after a dip in the infinity pool, a pink-trimmed, bright green napkin under a Sazerac, a trapunto-stitched quilt your great-granddaughter will still be using in her space pod.

So open your rooms to possibility, shake out any antiquated notions of what luxury linens are, and express yourself!

JANE SCOTT HODGES

A unique, Asian-inspired monogram emblazoned on the dinner napkin takes the table décor to the next level.

THE FANATIC

PASSION FOR THE ART OF LIVING WITH FINE LINENS

DEVOTEE, OBSESSED FAN, EXPERT WITNESS, FABRIC ADDICT. Call it what you will. When it comes to fine linens, I'm happy to wear the title.

I was hooked the moment I discovered a treasure trove left by my great-great-grandmother in the attic of our family home. I was just about to get married and had reached that age when you start to understand the value of tradition and of passing along important family history from one generation to the next. My great-great-grandmother's stash included lovely objects she had used daily, as well as for special occasions, and volumes of leather-bound journals, written to her daughter, my great-grandmother, full of beautifully penned wisdom and wonderful etchings. And when I saw that her exquisite hand-monogrammed linens were emblazoned with the same initials I would soon be using . . . well, the serendipity was hard to ignore. The initial spark from that encounter became a fast-growing interest, the interest became devotion, and the devotion led me to Eleanor Beard, the historic studio that became the basis for my business.

Eleanor Beard was a shrewd businesswoman, unique within her generation, who had figured out early on the benefits of reaching out and marketing directly to women. Her husband owned a general store, and with the Great Depression in full swing, he was often paid in wool by the local farmers who had no cash. The wool itself had little value, and so after cleaning and batting it, Eleanor took orders for quilts and commissioned local craftswomen, who would work from home, to make them. The gorgeous quilts became sought after in the luxury market, and soon, Eleanor opened her namesake studio, employing hundreds of talented needleworkers. The products expanded from quilts to include blanket covers, sheeting, table linens, bedclothes, and bath accessories—all of which stood apart from the mass-produced items found at department stores—to become family heirlooms that have been passed down from generation to generation. The success of the enterprise grew to include shops in New York,

My great-great-grandmother's sewing kit and heirloom linens sparked my interest in recreating vintage pieces for all to enjoy. The notion of linens being used by my ancestors and withstanding the test of time fascinated me.

Eleanor Beard Inc.

Chicago, and elsewhere, which Beard intended as social clubs where women could relax and socialize while they shopped.

After Beard passed away in 1951, the business sadly lost its bridge to the world outside of rural Kentucky, and it slowly disappeared from the marketplace. When I acquired the Eleanor Beard brand in 2002, the studio's name and what it stood for had all but disappeared. I was determined to bring Eleanor Beard back to its roots as a collective of skilled artisans creating one-of-a-kind pieces, and likewise to take inspiration from the Eleanor Beard salons for Leontine Linens, my flagship store in New Orleans. All Leontine Linens' pieces are designed by me and my talented team, working directly with clients in their homes or in the comfortable, unhurried setting of the salon, and are handmade in the original Kentucky studio where Eleanor Beard started it all. It was a singular joy to take on the legacy of this storied name and merge it with my company. I hope that Eleanor would be proud of the way I've continued to shine a spotlight on the talents of these amazing artisans.

My goal over the years has been to reestablish the important role linens play in living and entertaining, as crucial a part of the home as the rest of the décor we put so much thought into. And I don't plan on quitting until satin-stitched sheets, appliquéd coverlets, and mono-grammed napkins find their way into every home that aspires to be a showcase for gracious, inspired living.

Men had their clubs; ladies had Eleanor Beard. This window from the heyday of Eleanor Beard's Park Avenue salon was a sumptuous invitation to a place where women could relax, commune, and, of course, shop. As evidenced by the intricate handwork on the spread, the organza bed skirt, and the trapunto-quilted dressing gown and pillows, Eleanor Beard Studio's linens were chic and unmatched in "crafts(wo)manship."

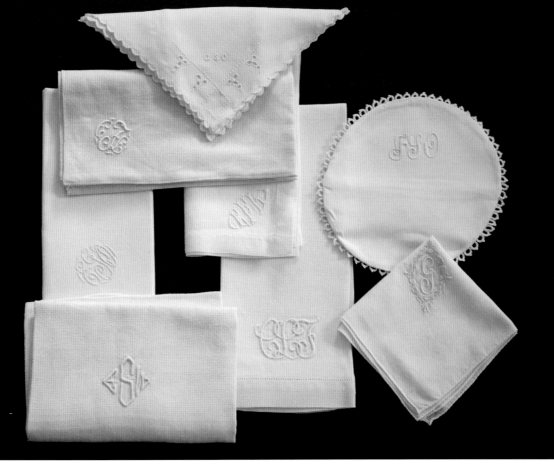

Above: The passion and perfection we put into
everything at Leontine Linens has earned us a lot of
press, but the real joy is getting to work so closely
with clients. The true reward is helping them to realize
their ideas and to create the individual pieces that add
that all-important finishing touch to their homes.
Opposite: Some of my great-great-grandmother's
treasures, which I discovered as a young woman. The
most valuable thing of all was the legacy she handed
down, and nothing attests to that more than her
personal items. While a photograph of her journal
captures a moment in time, heirloom linens tell the
deeper story—of her good taste, and how she lived
and entertained her family and friends. These little
pieces of her world moved me enough to dedicate
my life to reimagining the gracious, generous times in
which she lived.

DESIGNING WITH LEONTINE LINENS

ALEXA HAMPTON

I was first introduced to Leontine Linens by a beloved and esteemed client in New Orleans in the late 1990s. I met with Jane Scott over the client's dining room table, where we pored over her books of colored threads, examples of details and various materials brought for our consideration. The experience was amazing. First and foremost, the quality of the workmanship was exceptional. Our choices were also vast; but, one of the most thrilling parts of that meeting was the realization that we had stumbled upon lovely and capable collaborators. We weren't simply engaging a vendor; we were interacting with trained and talented partners. Ever since, my office has had a direct line established between us, our clients, and the tour de force that is Leontine Linens.

As a designer, I have three major directives at all times, regardless of the job at hand: I have to create a beautiful space; it has to fulfill its function; and it must provide pleasure and comfort to those who experience the interior. In this, Leontine Linens is my ally. One's bed and bath are, after all, locations where one can feel particularly vulnerable. (Nudity! Unconsciousness!) So, there, it is particularly important to have a rich tactile experience, one that displays elements as useful as they are stunning. Of course, my own bedding and towels are Leontine Linens, and so I feel I can speak with special authority about their products and the journey that ends with the arrival of a beautiful purple-bow—bedecked package of bespoke items. Heaven!

In this warm, inviting guest room, Alexa Hampton uses bordered shams, quilted spreads, and vibrant bolsters to tie together the beds and the patterned wall and rug. Opposite: Shams in a sweet floral print and ruffled trim up the romance of this canopied bed by Alexa Hampton.

THE DETAIL GEEK

MONOGRAMS, BORDERS, AND OTHER TECHNIQUES FOR EMBELLISHMENT

 THOSE WHO LOVE DETAILS are a devoted bunch, and the details of fine linens are worth the reverence. In the world of custom linens, quality fabrics such as linen, cotton, and silk can be woven as fine as gossamer or as hearty as burlap. These then form the base for the decorative embellishments that make your mark. In fact, embellishment on linen has evolved so much over the years—through both technical expertise and sheer imagination—that we have an amazing wealth of tactile and visual effects to choose from.

French knot and ring stitch bring a formal yet simple feel to a pillow's edge. Swiss fill will add dimension to white on white. Trapunto turns even the thinnest of fabrics substantial. Jacquard makes light play beautifully over a fabric's surface. These are just a taste of the possibilities.

And there are, of course, the monograms, which are particularly dear to my heart. Monograms can be as discreet as a subtle, single initial on the tucked corner of a handkerchief or as bold as a twelve-inch focal point in the center of a sham.

Once you see all the ways embellishment can make linens distinctive and unique, piece to piece, you'll understand why they're fast moving to the forefront of decorative decisions in home décor—and, more so, why finely rendered linens are a prominent topic in any conversation concerning how to transform "eating" into "having a meal," "sleep" into "reverie," and "washing" into "bathing."

Yes, indeed, exquisitely detailed linens turn life into living.

Previous pages: My own monogram—shown on my personal collection of table linens—takes on a variety of personalities, demonstrating the sheer multitude of designs available when selecting custom linens. Opposite: An antique linen cupboard provides an elegant place to house your collection of fine linens. The wide assortment of embroidery, appliqué, prints, and quilts is both a visual and a tactile feast.

THE MONOGRAM

Monograms can be rendered in as many styles as there are personalities. At Leontine Linens we have created hundreds of monogram styles, ranging from ornate calligraphic designs, which hark back to royal houses, to very simple letterforms that are more modern in spirit. We also love the challenge of coming up with something completely new. Dozens of different thread-work techniques can be employed to bring a monogram to life, whether it's a single letter, a cipher of two initials, or the traditional grouping of three letters. As for where you put it, again, there are no limits. Monograms can be embroidered or appliquéd in the traditional spots on pillows, top sheets, and napkins, or they can show up in more unexpected places, for instance, on the back of an upholstered dining chair or on a fabric bed crown.

Embroidered monograms for every need and taste. Clockwise, from top, left: A traditional three-letter monogram in Swiss fill embroidery; An intricate three-letter monogram with seed stitch detailing in which the letters read straight across; A cipher, two-letter monogram with seed stitch detail; Cocktail napkins with a custom ring stitch monogram; A telltale sign of custom work—a specialized detail, "Jr.," neatly tucked into the center letter; An embroidered name in place of initials.

Above: An intricate emerald-green monogram
embroidered on crisp white linen—a refreshing
complement to a beautiful place setting.
Opposite: Appliqué monograms can be
rendered in so many styles that there is always an
opportunity to play them off other elements in
the room. Here, Cathy Kincaid Hudson employs
a diamond-shaped monogram that echoes the
shape of the headboard.

DESIGNING WITH MONOGRAMS

GWEN DRISCOLL

Creating spaces that exhibit a client's personal style is central in my design process. I love monograms and always have, from the first monogrammed sweater I received for Christmas long ago! Whether it's a beautiful set of monogrammed napkins handed down from Granny or newly created bedding with your custom monogram, it's the perfect way to subtly say, "I belong here, and my home is open to entertain, love, and host you."

A signature of my design is a refined and clean palette. This allows for striking focal points in each space. A monogram is my first choice to create that in bed, bath, entertaining spaces, and anywhere else it's appropriate. I build a strong design aesthetic for each project, combining my client's style with my design expertise. Monograms, without a doubt, are the most notable way to lend a personal touch. It's your signature and a lovely finishing detail.

Creative, geometric monograms with a modern flair are perfect for cocktail napkins. Versatile monograms are key in the dining room, for use on every type of china and glassware in your butler's pantry. I love to create a succinct monogram design for the bedroom and bathroom. Each should be unique but still have a common language that relates them in the most personal way.

Monograms have been with us for ages. My heart always sinks when a client expresses they're not for them. I then focus on creating a fabulous border or geometric appliqué that will still reflect their personal best.

The beautiful work of hand-done monograms warrants display, so don't hide them in a drawer. These Lucite boxes make a collection of cocktail napkins and guest towels both precious and accessible.

DESIGNING WITH BORDERS

DAVID KLEINBERG

I really don't care for monograms except on the cuff of a man's shirt—where they are small and discreet and needed to avoid confusion when sent to the laundry. Perhaps as a holdover from a somewhat liberal upbringing in a modernist house during the late 1960s and early 1970s, I find the idea of a monogram slightly self-conscious, and even boastful. A recurring theme in my decoration is pattern-making through unexpected sources, such as texture and interesting graphic elements. Monograms distract from this decorative course and interrupt the strong graphic statement I'm always seeking.

As a designer, I much prefer to create refined, custom appliqués or elegant, hand-embroidered borders. My eye is more drawn to a beautiful flange in an accent color on the edge of a boudoir pillow or a handsome, inset appliqué border on a European sham than to a bold statement in the middle.

I prefer the subtlety of these techniques and appreciate the handwork involved. My bedrooms tend to be quiet in their decoration, and I find monograms to be that slight bit of extra noise that the bed linens don't need.

In this bedroom by David Kleinberg, a classic appliqué border detail on the shams, pillowcases, and flat sheet add finesse and finish without distracting from the room's clean, modern aesthetic. When you see what a skilled designer can do with linen details, it's hard to imagine a room like this working as well with just plain bedding. Following pages: The delicate appliqué border that details the edges of the blanket cover and French cases is custom tailored to complement the serene lavender accents of the bedroom. Design by Amanda Nisbet.

A close look at these lovely monograms reveals what hand embroidery can do that a machine never could. Above: A framed monogram on a linen napkin shows a Swiss fill technique with a seed-stitch detail. Opposite, top: Another example of Swiss fill embroidery. Opposite, bottom: An ivory monogram in a ring stitch (also called chain stitch) technique on pale blue linen.

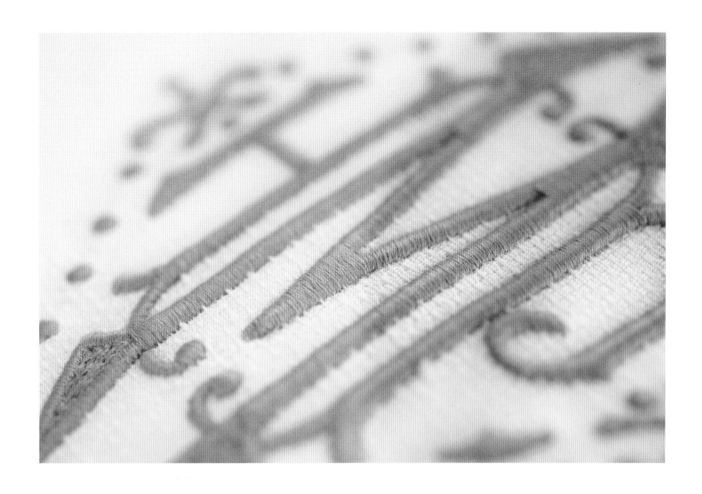

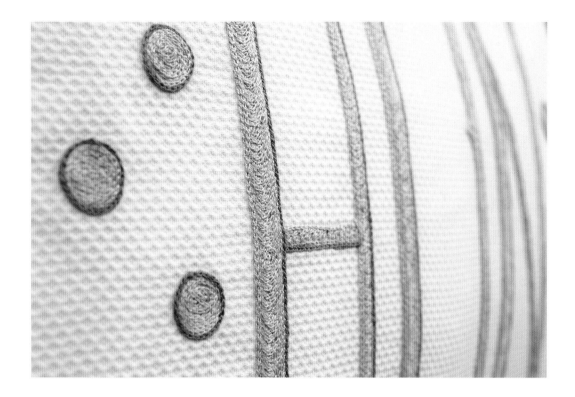

Exquisitely rendered embroidery details transform linens to the realm of the sublime, allowing them to seamlessly complement their surroundings. Opposite: Two-tone Swiss fill embroidery in pink and olive threads dances across powdery blue sateen sheets. Top: Shaded ring stitch embroidery in two shades of blue adds a highly raised surface texture to classic pique fabric. Bottom: Ring stitch can also be executed in the most delicate of hand, as shown on this scalloped-edged placemat and matching napkin.

Though similar, these scrolling designs illustrate the difference between embroidery and appliqué. Both techniques allow for an infinite variety of patterns. Above: Appliqué, shown on the bedspread, involves embroidering a trim fabric onto the base fabric in the chosen design. Opposite: Distinct from appliqué, embroidery can be thought of as an "all thread" technique. Here, a detail of embroidered borders done in ring stitch and Swiss fill.

A combination of incredibly detailed embroidery and cutwork is often referred to as "Swiss trim" because of its European origin. You are not likely to find a more elegant addition to your linen collection—this embellishment is the ultimate indulgence.

THE MEANING OF HANDMADE

With more and more manufacturers searching for ways to make their products special, the term *handmade* has become overused and misunderstood to the point that it has lost its true meaning and impact.

In terms of the linen world, *handmade* should refer to only two techniques: literally, sewn by hand with a needle and thread, or sewn by a hand-guided machine.

Probably the best-known applications to custom linens are monograms, borders, and embroidery. For the most part, when these are offered through catalogue businesses or home sections in large retail operations, they are executed with a computerized embroidery machine, using patterns that have been "digitized" with embroidery software. As far as I know, computers don't have hands, and so while it may be touted as "custom made," digital manufacture cannot be considered handmade. At my shop, Leontine Linens, each design is first hand drawn by our artisans. A majority of the construction is accomplished on a hand-guided sewing machine, which allows greater scope in the composition and greater sophistication in the execution of the design. The expert hand of a seamstress guides the needle of her embroidery machine, allowing for detail and self-correction that is not possible with a digitized system. Following this stage, many of the finishing details, including appliqué, hand turning of the piece, button closures, and the final few hemming whipstitches, are done completely by hand.

Truly handmade linens will not only retain their value due to the labor that goes into each and every piece, they will also hold up better over time.

Once you're hooked on the difference handmade makes, you may want to start searching out rare handwork pieces. The best places to find these are in European flea markets, from reputable dealers who specialize in linens, and on your travels, especially through the American heartland, where estate sales will often yield generations-old pieces that have been lovingly maintained.

Previous pages: Antique monogram books are the perfect sources for the type of intricate designs that were only possible before the age of digitizing and machine embroidery. Hand-drawn renderings can be used to reinterpret these designs in your own initials, and then to serve as the pattern for custom embroidery. Thread skeins are the reference from which to choose your embroidery color. Above: Big, singular bed-width pillows with perfectly sized and placed monograms hold their own against the trapunto-quilted duvets folded at the foot in this cozy bedroom by Cathy Kincaid Hudson. Opposite: This monogram in ring stitch employs the entire pillow as a canvas for its linking letterforms.

THE HISTORY BUFF

THE TROUSSEAU AND COLLECTING FINE LINENS

WHILE THE AESTHETIC DELIGHTS of custom linens are formidable, understanding the history behind them can add immeasurably to their impact.

Customizing linens for both personal and public use goes back to the fourteenth century. Before the advent of mass production, bedding and tablecloths that were handwoven from finer, laboriously produced materials such as linen and silk were naturally more precious, and they were tended to with the kind of devotion we wouldn't see today, even in the finest homes. They were often the only things of value that a family of modest means possessed, and handing them down through generations was the equivalent of passing along a monetary inheritance.

The development of fine linens can be attributed to two significant aspects of our cultural history: the trousseau and the monogram.

The trousseau comprised the household linens a bride would take to her new home. This was distinct from the traditional dowry offered to the husband by the bride's family, as a trousseau consisted of items the new family would use for living and entertaining. For a girl back then, the creation of a trousseau began when she was barely out of pigtails, as it took years for her and the other women of the family to hand make the number of sheets, tablecloths, etc., needed for comfortable living.

Most trousseau pieces were monogrammed, a way to signify ownership. But what began as a perfunctory security measure executed in a simple, typically red stitch soon turned into the elaborate marks of royal houses that inspire the detailed monograms of today.

For the die-hard linen-history buff, nothing beats collecting rare, antique pieces. If you've never held up a perfectly preserved, gossamer sheet to the sunlight at a Paris flea market or run your hand over silk quilted with tiny cross-stitches that took a turn-of-the-century artisan two years to make, you don't know what you're missing.

There are no hard and fast rules when it comes to your trousseau. It can be what you make it. For example, a vintage trunk filled with sheet sets and table settings, some old and some new, to outfit your new home for personal use and entertaining.

THE TROUSSEAU

Something old, something new, something borrowed, something blue—who knows just where or how long ago that rhyme originated, but the tradition of the trousseau it references continues to be unlocked by young brides today. A trousseau is the collection of household linens that a young woman acquires, or in some cases makes, in anticipation of her marriage. The concept of thoughtfully assembling a young girl's linens for her future transcends both time and culture, as well it should. No matter how seasoned or worldly you imagine yourself to be, hitching up with a life partner introduces a whole slew of unknowns into your world. The trousseau is a way for your loved ones to let you know that they'll be there for steadiness when all those vagaries come flying at you, and to let your spouse know that your family is supportive of the partnership upon which you're embarking.

The concept of the trousseau has had to keep pace with the ever-expanding range of marriage styles, but it nonetheless has retained its most comforting aspects. Pieces handed down for generations will always be an important part, as they echo the voices of those who have been through all of this before you—each thread in a quilted blanket or embroidered set of linen sheets carrying lessons on how to move though cohabitation successfully.

But modern times mean modern ideas, and twenty-first-century trousseaux reflect the taste of the married couple much more than that of the relatives putting it together. So no need to fret that you'll be getting a trunk full of sheets that won't work with your bleached-oak bedroom furniture, or quilts that look uncomfortably out of place draped over an Eames lounge. With custom linens now so incredibly varied and adaptable, how you outfit your home and entertain your friends will be one of the things you and your other half shouldn't have to "discuss."

GETTING MARRIED IS A PERFECT TIME TO SPOIL YOURSELF WITH BEAUTIFUL LINENS

DARCY MILLER

- Start your registry early—ideally, six months before your wedding date. That way, you can include items that could even be used at the wedding itself. A great example is a handkerchief you could have embroidered with blue thread to carry as your "something blue."

- If you and your spouse-to-be have different tastes in linens, don't argue about it! When in doubt, go with white. It's a timeless option, sure to please long after you've stopped being obsessed with the color of the season.

- Introduce patterns and colors in the form of blankets and shams. You can get very creative. Plus, it's easier to change up pillows and throws than to repaint the room.

- No doubt you'll want to register for a cashmere throw to complete the look of a favorite sofa or chair, but be sure to also register for a cotton one. When you're lounging around and want to feel cozy, you'll be glad the softer option is on hand.

- Be sure to touch and feel the linens when registering in-store. You don't want to register for itchy sheets or stiff bath towels, no matter how gorgeous—you'll regret it!

- Register for two sets of sheets per bed in your home. You always want to have a spare, when your main set is in the laundry—or, worse, stained or damaged beyond repair. The same holds true for bath linens: two complete sets per bathroom.

- Runners and placemats are great ways to dress up your table (and take a lot less ironing than big cloths). Runners are also great for side tables, mantels, etc.

- When it comes to napkins, you want to go for two sets to meet different needs. One set should be durable and stain-resistant for everyday use. The other should be a high-quality set you'll pull out for those special dinner parties. The same holds true for kitchen towels. Most should be workhorses, but you can add in a few show ponies for when you're entertaining guests.

- Embroidering your initials onto any linen kicks it up several notches. And think outside the powder-room towel! Any linen you love can surely be monogrammed. One of my favorite wedding gifts was a surprise from a friend: bathmats that featured the monogram used on our invitations.

Previous pages: A more casual trousseau could be a unique suitcase (or collection of them) housing favorite pieces of jewelry you found on trips with your boyfriend-now-husband; your mom's scarves, which you borrowed so often she finally just let you have them; and keepsakes from relatives.

Opposite: Linen pieces commissioned for your wedding don't have to be boxed up and stored away like your gown. This classic hemstitched table runner with your new monogram is designed not only to become an heirloom, but also to be used as a go-to piece for both casual and formal dinners, serving as a reminder of that magical day each time you lay it out.

COLLECTING & USING
FINE LINENS

Few avid collectors have the room to perma-
nently showcase everything they acquire, and so
for most, the satisfaction comes in the search.
Thus, hunting for antique linens can be a more
enjoyable endeavor for the collector, as linens
come with the added bonus of being useful.

Yes, antiques are often more delicate than
newer linens, but that doesn't mean they can't
be put to task: draped over a daybed or chair
that's less frequently used (and one the cat
stays off of!), or folded up at the foot of your
bed and employed only on the occasional evening you want to tuck yourself under something
with the weight of history. And vintage sheets
work well in guest rooms that get less traffic
than other bedrooms.

Of course, as with your other collectables,
you have the option of making a more formal
display. After all, when *handmade* was the only
made, the amount of labor that went into a
linen piece warranted its position as a work
of art—beyond its practical duty. A great old
monogram, its letterforms rendered in a style no
longer found, can be wrapped around a canvas
and placed in a shadow box. Vintage linen handkerchiefs can be displayed on a silver dressing-
table tray. And some older quilts and coverlets
can even be hung on the wall like tapestries, as
they were often rendered in a singular, centered
motif, rather than a repetitive pattern.

The fact that bed and table linens will
always be a ubiquitous aspect of daily life make
them something that can truly satisfy a collecting bug.

This tassel design is a modern interpretation of an heirloom pattern, dating
back to the 1930s, uncovered in the Eleanor Beard Studio archives. Lest
you be tempted to store your fine linens away, remember that they are
meant to be used and loved. This satin quilt in the dreamiest of blues
makes a sojourn on the porch that much more special.

LINEN TREASURES

GAY WIRTH

As a child, I loved to open my grandmother's drawer filled with lovely handkerchiefs and touch them. She used them daily. There my journey of discovering the world of vintage linens began. Later, when staying with French friends, I learned that beautiful things scream to be appreciated, loved, and used.

Linen treasures can be found everywhere—in antique shops, flea markets, and garage sales. There is no right or wrong in deciding which ones to buy. The most important thing is to learn what you like and not be afraid to *use* it. I find that natural fabric offers the best quality. The heavy, natural linen sheets are as wonderful as those with the finest thread count. One has texture, while the other is soft to the touch.

I prefer hand stitching on the linens. The initials on the sheets, napkins, tablecloths, torchons, etc., represent a culture of family. In Normandy, when a grandmother's lifestyle became limited, her job would be to design and hand stitch the linens for her grandchildren's trousseaux, placing their initials on each piece. As I use my vintage linens, I can just feel those grandmothers' love, and I cannot imagine living without it.

A collection of Gay Wirth's vintage linens, collected over various travels, are thoughtfully stored in an antique armoire at her New Orleans shop.

THE LEGACY OF HEIRLOOM LINENS

LAURA VINROOT POOLE

I am named after my grandmother, my great-aunt, and my great-grandmother, none of whom I had the chance to know before they were gone. What I do know are the drawers full of family linens they left behind for me—talismans that give me clarity and strength.

There are hand-stitched handkerchiefs that sit in my pocketbook and comfort me when I weep. There are neatly stacked hand towels in my powder room from my grandmother's trousseau that remind me how young she was when she married at twenty-one. There are hemstitched dinner napkins that sit on our laps at every Sunday dinner. The pale pink cocktail napkins with appliquéd baby chicks have dabbed the edges of my gimlets as I'm sure they did my grandmother's favorite cocktail each day at 5:00 p.m. The beauty of inherited linens is the inevitability that if I care for them the way the women before me cared for them, they will last for my daughter's family and for those who follow her. And, as we did before her, she and her family will hold the hands of those for whom she was named.

Mixing the old with the new helps to highlight the beauty in both. The delicate white monogram on an heirloom handkerchief is luxury at its most discreet.

Above: A sleek vertical monogram is the perfect choice for a modern gentleman. Opposite: A pincushion filled with Mardi Gras pins is displayed on a backdrop of printed and monogrammed handkerchiefs.

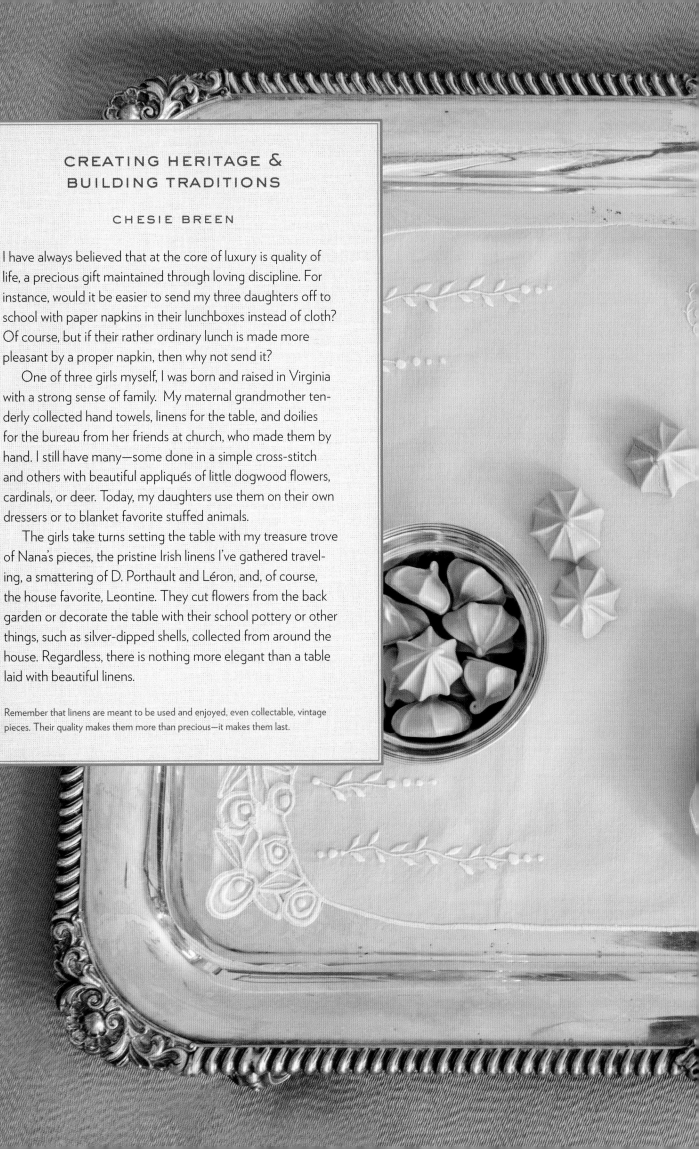

CREATING HERITAGE & BUILDING TRADITIONS

CHESIE BREEN

I have always believed that at the core of luxury is quality of life, a precious gift maintained through loving discipline. For instance, would it be easier to send my three daughters off to school with paper napkins in their lunchboxes instead of cloth? Of course, but if their rather ordinary lunch is made more pleasant by a proper napkin, then why not send it?

One of three girls myself, I was born and raised in Virginia with a strong sense of family. My maternal grandmother tenderly collected hand towels, linens for the table, and doilies for the bureau from her friends at church, who made them by hand. I still have many—some done in a simple cross-stitch and others with beautiful appliqués of little dogwood flowers, cardinals, or deer. Today, my daughters use them on their own dressers or to blanket favorite stuffed animals.

The girls take turns setting the table with my treasure trove of Nana's pieces, the pristine Irish linens I've gathered traveling, a smattering of D. Porthault and Léron, and, of course, the house favorite, Leontine. They cut flowers from the back garden or decorate the table with their school pottery or other things, such as silver-dipped shells, collected from around the house. Regardless, there is nothing more elegant than a table laid with beautiful linens.

Remember that linens are meant to be used and enjoyed, even collectable, vintage pieces. Their quality makes them more than precious—it makes them last.

THE DREAMER

BUILDING YOUR BED LAYER BY LAYER

*D*REAMING DOESN'T NECESSARILY REQUIRE SLUMBER, but it does require a sanctuary of sorts. Dreamers are adept at creating these peace-of-mind habitats, places that are serene but not boring, quiet enough for contemplation yet rich enough to get the juices flowing. And nothing is more essential to outfitting a peaceful place for inspiration than the luxury of fine bed linens

Building your bed begins with sheets in pampering fabrics such as pure linen, cotton percale or sateen, and luxurious silk. The fitted sheet, flat sheet, and pillowcases, whether you prefer them buttery soft or starched and crisp, provide the tactile pleasure that transforms the overnight hours into a good night's sleep. The bedcover can be chosen and changed to suit any mood: a pique blanket cover warm yet light as air; a duvet with comforting but not confining weight; a quilt rendered in soothing, pillowy waves; a throw in the finest cashmere or wool, in a stimulating hue to add color to your reveries. Pillows cradle your head as you slumber. Big and downy, they come in a variety of other shapes and sizes: neck rolls, bolsters, body pillows wide as the bed and broad as possibility.

Revel in the bedding choices that allow you to build the perfect vessel to transport you from night to day. Both visually and to the touch, a beautiful place of respite is the dreamer's greatest joy and source of inspiration.

Opposite and following pages: Take me to dreamland.
Appliquéd vines on the blanket cover and pillow shams
complete this richly patterned room by Alexa Hampton.

SHEETS AND PILLOWCASES

Basics: The basic sheet set is comprised of a fitted sheet, a flat sheet, and corresponding pillowcases.

Sheet Sizing: Sheet sets are sized to correspond with the various bed sizes. However, it's crucial to measure your mattress, as many of today's mattresses are so deep that some fitted sheets will not stretch over them. Many manufacturers will designate sets as "extra deep" to address this problem.

Not Fit for Fitted: Some don't like fitted sheets due to the elastic, which can lose its tautness over time and often rides up if the sheet isn't deep enough. The alternative is to use a flat sheet and tuck it in tightly.

Pillowcases: The term *pillowcase* refers to the standard, side-opening "envelope" that a pillow is slipped into. Cases come in sizes corresponding to pillow sizes: standard, queen, and king.

French Cases: French cases, aka shams, are an alternative to pillowcases and open in the back rather than the side. Shams are used both for sleeping and as decorative additions; thus, they tend to come in a wider array of fabrics than pillowcases do.

Fabric Quality: The sheets and pillowcases are the parts of the bed you spend most of the time in contact with, so the touch and feel of the fabric is of the utmost importance. Thread count has become an unreliable method for designating quality, so pay attention instead to the type of fabric and weave. Cotton percale is cool and crisp. Cotton sateen is silky. Pure linen is starchy but will soften with age and use. Silk is another option and has a luxurious look and feel.

Crisp cotton sheet sets, stacked and wrapped with a matching pillowcase, allow for easy identification when stored.

If only in a dream . . . Inspired by D. Porthault's
bright and modern print, this daybed nestled
on a summer balcony offers sanctuary from the
real world. Colors, patterns, and appliqué and
embroidery details are married to create a bright,
bohemian, and chic perch.

BLANKET COVERS

Basics: The blanket cover is the most versatile piece for the bed, and it is the first building block when designing a bed. This is the most visible part of a bed's look: it is the largest expanse of fabric that shows, and thus it warrants the most attention.

Over-Pillow Length: A blanket cover can be made with extra length so as to neatly cover the sleeping pillows. This alleviates the need for decorative shams and gives a simple, tailored look.

Reverse Tuck: A reverse tuck, or reverse sham, is an option that provides a more decorative finish than an over-pillow length. The reverse tuck envelops the sleeping pillows from the top and sometimes features a decorative border on the outside edge.

An Alternative to a Duvet Cover: If you find keeping the duvet cover neat to be a frustrating challenge, forego it altogether and simply layer your duvet under your blanket cover.

QUILTS

Basics: Quilts are layering pieces that can be placed on top of the blanket cover for extra warmth. When not in use, quilts can be folded at the foot of the bed.

White-on-White Quilts: The stitching technique used to decorate quilts of a single fabric exterior, by either outlining the elements of a print (such as a chintz) or embellishing a solid fabric, is referred to as a "white on white" technique. The quilts of the historic Eleanor Beard Studio are of this style.

Pieced Quilts: More commonly found are what's known as pieced quilts, where different fabrics have been sewn together to create a patchwork pattern that can range in complexity, from a simple design to a more intricate arrangement.

DUVET COVERS

Basics: The duvet cover is the fabric "envelope" into which a down duvet (often referred to as a "comforter") is slipped. A duvet cover often replaces or is used in conjunction with a blanket cover. Designed to protect the down duvet, it also serves as decoration.

Sizing a Duvet Cover: The duvet cover should be made to fit your insert. Duvets come in many shapes and sizes, and good fit is important so that the inserts do not shift or bunch inside.

Duvet Cover Choice: Look for a duvet cover with a zipper closure rather than buttons. You'll thank me every time you launder the cover and need to reinsert the duvet. You'll also like that the duvet doesn't sneak out between the buttons.

An Obedient Duvet: I recommend putting ties on the corners of your duvet and corresponding ties or loops on the inside corners of the duvet cover. This allows you to tie the duvet in place, which will eliminate shifting.

Designers will often turn to fine linens to throw a curveball into a room's decor, in this case quite literally. Opposite: A scalloped bedspread becomes a playmate for the bed's whimsical posts. Design by Charlotte Moss. Following pages: Scrolling appliqués and a festoon-bordered quilt move in rhythm with the baroque headboard and ivy vines on the walls. Design by Rob Southern. Pages 80–81: Serenity defined—a crisp percale duvet cover and French cases in classic white cotton, marked with the Addison monogram in a subtle shade of sage green, create the perfect nest for those lazy Sundays when you are granted the luxury to linger in bed a few extra hours. Design by Elizabeth Elsey.

UNDERSTANDING DOWN PRODUCTS AND DUVETS

With so many alternatives to down available, it's important to understand the benefits of choosing the finest down products for both duvets and pillows.

For those not "down with down," let's start with the basics: Down is the soft, fluffy undercoat of a goose or duck's feathers. Goose down is more expensive than duck down, and both are much more expensive than feather. Feathers are relatively inexpensive because they're heavier and don't insulate nearly as well. Because the mechanical process used to sort down is not perfect, down, feather, and fiber (broken pieces of down and feather mixed) are all present to some degree in products sold as "down." The advantages of down over synthetics are numerous, and, thus, the reason it costs more.

INSULATION: It's not the down itself that creates the insulation, but rather the tiny air pockets trapped by the down fibers. Nature has created the perfect insulation in the birds that produce natural down, and modern science is still trying to catch up with polyester and other down-like materials.

BREATHABILITY: Down, being a natural fiber, allows water vapor to pass through it without letting warmth escape. This means that moisture is wicked away from the sleeper, enabling the body to effortlessly regulate temperature.

LIGHTNESS: Down requires far less material (by weight) to achieve a certain level of insulating power than manmade or alternative materials. Nights are more restful when you're not weighed down or restricted in your movement.

CLING: You know how some duvets have a tendency to get lumpy? This is due to poor "cling." Down with a lot of cling will stay evenly in place on top of the sleeper, rather than shifting within the duvet's chamber. Cling is either specific to the species of goose, as in genuine eiderdown, or is found only in very mature down. In general, it is expensive to process down with high-clinging ability.

CLEANLINESS: The final measure of down quality is cleanliness. High-quality down is sanitized to eliminate bacteria and then specially treated to prevent future growth of bacteria, mold, and mildew. While the process is thorough, it is very gentle, ensuring that the down maintains its original softness and resiliency.

Gerrie Bremermann lightens the heft of this modern four-poster by introducing a fluffy duvet in a soft hue with a scalloped edge. The trim on the coverlet and shams is appliquéd to match.

THE BED SKIRT

Basics: Also called a "dust ruffle," the bed skirt, one of the finishing decorations of the bed, elevates the ensemble. It's also practical for concealing items stored under the bed.

Styles: Bed skirts come in many styles, which fall into two main groups: gathered and tailored. A gathered skirt gives a fuller, feminine look, while a tailored one lays flat with decorative box pleats.

THE BOX SPRING COVER

Basics: A no-fuss, tailored alternative to the bed skirt, a box spring cover is essentially a tailored fitted sheet that covers the box spring in a plain or decorative fabric. The benefit is an upholstered look that is very sophisticated. The drawback, of course, is that any items stored under the bed will be visible.

Bed skirts work in tandem with the rest of the linens to help set the tone for the room. Above: A box spring cover is the perfect option to highlight a decorative wood frame. Bottom: Sharper, tailored skirts work with simpler or more contemporary looks. Opposite: Generous volumes of fabric lend a romantic, indulgent feel in a room by MMR Interiors.

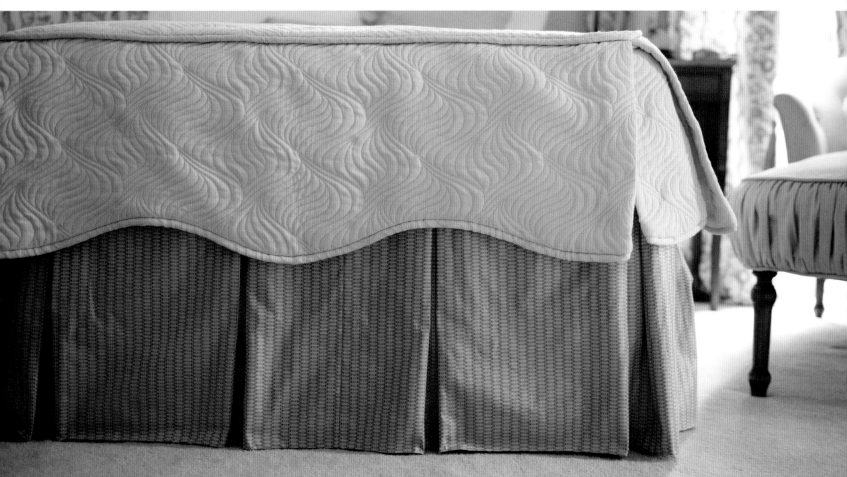

FRENCH CASE RECOMMENDATIONS
FOR BED SIZES

There's a fine balance between form and function when selecting the pillow shapes and sizes to combine on your bed. French cases, also called shams, are the decorative covers used to adorn the pillows that decorate the bed. Most people are familiar with king and standard, the widely available sizes. Less common sizes include the body pillow (twenty by sixty inches), Euro (short for European, twenty-six by twenty-six inches), and boudoir (twelve by sixteen inches). A bolster pillow is cylindrical in shape and named for its typical function of providing support on a bed or sofa. It works well as a decorative layering piece and is available in a wide array of custom sizes, the most common being the neck roll (five by sixteen inches). Before you get lost in a sea of pillows, here are some of my favorite arrangements for each bed size.

TWIN:

- I recommend a king sham, as the ends of the pillow will align perfectly with the width of the mattress for a very clean look.

- For a small accent pillow, a neck roll is the perfect proportion to sit in front of the decorative king sham. I also love accenting with a wedge pillow, especially in a child's room where the bed may be used for reading or homework.

QUEEN/FULL:

- For a dramatic look that creates a focal point, a pair of Euro shams, with a vibrant monogram or border, is the way to go. In fact, I sometimes prefer an oversized monogram on a pair of Euros, which makes a much stronger impact than a monogrammed blanket cover, which does not catch your eye when you walk into a room.

- For a layered look, I love two Euros with either two standards stacked in front or a single king, centered.

KING:

- Three Euro shams are a must in order to give the head of the bed ample coverage. Euro shams have a wonderful proportion on a king bed, which is very wide; they add a nicely proportioned height to the overall ensemble. You can stop there, or add another layer of, most commonly, a pair of king shams or a triplet of standard shams.

- I love a body pillow centered in front of the Euro shams. It creates a unified look, especially when you tie in the border and monogram elements that have been used on the other pieces of the ensemble.

Custom shams are the finishing touch to the perfectly made bed. Top: European shams provide the backdrop for the king shams and wedge pillow. Bottom: A combination of various sizes, heights, and widths make for an indulgent bed by Alexa Hampton.

PILLOW SIZES AND RECOMMENDATIONS

ELIZABETH MAYHEW

The number of pillows you have and how you arrange them can drastically change the style of your bed. For example, two standard pillows laid flat on a mattress will look much more modern, monastic, and streamlined than the more romantic pillow arrangement of two standard pillows standing behind two standard shams, with one decorative square pillow (or boudoir) and one neck roll centered in front. For a tailored look, start by propping two European shams up against your headboard, and then add two standard pillows and two boudoir pillows, centered in front. If you want a bohemian look, loosely toss pillows of various shapes and sizes onto your bed, making sure they are covered in different but coordinated designs.

Pillows do need fluffing, especially if they are down filled, but please don't overpuff them! You don't want them to look perfect. Also, I am not a big fan of the "karate chop." This is when you fluff the pillow, put it where you want it, and then, with your hand, karate chop the center of the top edge (you can often witness salespeople in furniture showrooms implementing this technique). It's better to fluff the pillow and then, while holding the top two corners, toss it where you want it to go. If it doesn't dimple in the fall, gently push in the middle sides, so that the pillow has a natural, relaxed look.

Elegant European shams are a simple accent to the antique French headboard and cornice in a room by Melissa Rufty. Opposite: Layers of sheeting, French cases, and a blanket cover create the most inviting of spaces. The intricate border on the flat sheet is not wasted when folded back below the French cases in this bedroom by Mary McDonald.

Bolsters and body pillows are an easy way to play and transform the bedroom. Above: The neck roll is a miniature match to the larger sham for a uniform look in a room by Alexa Hampton. Opposite, top: In Frances Schultz's charming cottage bedroom, a bed-width body pillow makes a striking impact but keeps the bed's design scheme simple.

Opposite, bottom: Liz Caan uses playfully stacked neck roll pillows to anchor the monogrammed Euro shams. Following pages: Cathy Kincaid Hudson uses bolsters to pop a bright spark of yellow into her airy blue-and-white bedroom.

CREATING A NEST FOR GUESTS

A favorite client imparted to me long ago the importance of placing your very best linens in the guest room as an assurance that your guests will be nothing but spoiled. High-quality bedding is the gracious way to welcome anyone spending the night in your home. Here are some tips for making their stay as luxurious as it would be in the finest hotel suite.

- Be prepared with an amply stocked closet containing extra blankets and pillows.
- Plan on two sleeping pillows per person. It's a nice idea to have two firm and two soft so that guests can mix and match to their preference.

- Do not overburden guests with too many items on the bed. A simple blanket cover with a pair of decorative shams, or even a reverse tuck, ensures a short journey to bed at the end of a long day of travel.
- Consider a sheet set that uses shams instead of cases to cover the sleeping pillows; shams are tidier as well as easier to neaten up in the morning.
- Percale is my go-to choice for fabric in the guest room; its appeal is much more universal than that of sateen, silk, or even linen.
- A beautiful satin quilt folded on a chair back or at the foot of the bed is the perfect invitation for an afternoon nap.

Dressing the guest room does not necessarily mean emblazoning your monogram on your linens—"custom" does not have to mean "monogrammed." Above: Simple piping and bands complete the look of the bright green guest room by Margaux Interiors. Simply toss the monogrammed neck roll into the closet when guests arrive. Opposite: Linen French cases with an embroidered border are a subtle nod to the wallpaper and bed skirt, for a truly finished look in a room by Matthew Carter.

THE WELL-APPOINTED GUESTROOM

SUZANNE LOVELL

"The ornament of a house is the friends who frequent it."

—Ralph Waldo Emerson

Creating a lovely guestroom, where your friends and family feel welcome, isn't hard. It just takes thought, planning, and a little role-play. Start by thinking about what you would wish for if you yourself were coming into that same guest room, tired and exhausted after a long trip. You would want it to be gracious and super easy to understand. You would want the space to be light and bright. It should make you smile with the welcoming message to stay, relax, and enjoy the beautiful surroundings.

Guestroom bedding should be crisp, with enough downy pillows to give your guests options for sleeping. Build your bed in layers. Use fresh white sheets in natural fibers, a coverlet, and a down duvet for those who like extra warmth. Have fun with color accents, employing them in contrasting edges or embroidered embellishments on the blanket cover and pillow shams. As a final touch, pamper your guests with monogrammed neck rolls or small boudoir pillows, and lay a monogrammed bathrobe at the end of the bed. Who wouldn't want to check in?

This guest suite gives visitors plenty of space and privacy. Large enough for a seating area, kept in neutral tones, and with classic linear appliqué borders on the custom linens, this guest space designed by Suzanne Lovell is a retreat in which anyone can relax.

A pared-down take on layering—standard shams behind boudoir pillows, all with an elegant, single-letter monogram to accent the classic floral headboard—in a bedroom by Rob Southern.

GROWING UP WITH LINENS

There's a fine line between indulging and spoiling, and with two of my own still partially in the nest, I'm not one to judge. So I like to think of outfitting children's rooms with custom linens as a way to help them develop their sense of personal style and to help me learn their likes and dislikes.

Linen embellishments adapt so well to the playfulness inherent in children's spaces that you wonder if maybe the whole idea was born there. A bouncy bed is one of the first toys a child discovers, and so let it be just that by bordering the comforter with a big bright stripe and appliquéing a whimsical monogram in the center. Whether predominantly pink, true blue, or a riot of neons, custom linens will always play well with everything else in the room.

Nurseries, of course, are a different story, as babies can't express a preference for apple green over robin's egg blue. But they certainly can communicate their preference for fabric, so all the more reason to indulge them with the finest, softest natural materials. High quality non-synthetic fabrics, such as pure cotton batiste and percale, will also hold up to more frequent washing. And that hand-embroidered monogram on the bumper might just be helping little Emma develop a taste for the finer things, something that will prove useful when she becomes president.

Below: When do babies start dreaming? The moment you set them down in a crib outfitted with custom linens. Opposite: Children's rooms are places in which the linens can be playful, with bright colors and whimsical monograms.

TIPS FOR CHILDREN'S ROOMS

AMANDA NISBET

- Remember whose space it is: Comfort, color, and whimsy are the key design elements that I gravitate to for children's bed linens, without letting things get too immature or kitschy. I love bright color and an overall design as cheerful as the child who inhabits the room.

- Consider adding monograms: Children love to see their names emblazoned on everything from jewelry to journals and clothes, so customizing their linens with their names or monograms is a great way to add a little luxury to their spaces. Delicate scripted letters for a girl's room, or graphic, lowercase block letters for something more masculine and modern for a boy's. Either way, I make sure it's something that speaks to their youth without being too "cute."

- Make sure the design will last longer than their shoes and clothes: When investing in doing a child's room well, make the design an overall one that will grow with the child and won't fall prey to dating itself.

Simply bordered white linens and a delicate print on the duvet make this cocoon of pink even more inviting in a room by Ruthie Sommers. Opposite: With a whimsical headboard, there is no better complement to fuchsia-trimmed bedding than a frilly single initial. Design by Amanda Nisbet.

THE TRADITIONALIST-WITH-A-TWIST

REINTERPRETING CLASSIC LINENS IN MODERN WAYS

"EVOLUTION, NOT REVOLUTION" is the motto of those who like a little rhubarb in their strawberry pie. While there are some things that can't be improved upon—such as airy white linen sheets on a hot New Orleans summer night—there are others that can show respect for tried-and-true values while injecting them with a wink. The traditionalist-with-a-twist understands the delight in reinterpreting something as classic as fine bed linens in a modern way, because what you end up with is both stimulating and reassuring at the same time.

A mahogany-paneled bedroom, its imposing four-poster bed usually dressed in white, becomes something entirely fresh when that bed is dressed in an ecru coverlet with a fuchsia monogram. Your reserved grandmother's whitewashed-cane daybed becomes a hangout for your decidedly unreserved daughter when the linen sheets go from eyelet to eye-pop. And a duvet appliquéd with a big double-stripe border is just the thing to wake up that serene Pierre Deux–fabric wall covering that you just can't seem to part with.

So whether injecting less expected touches into the traditional or bringing traditional accents into a more modern scenario, remember that it's your confidence that will allow you to make your mark.

Designer Beth Webb uses layer upon layer of a classic Greek key motif in a mix of neutral and blue. Mixing in different versions of the same pattern is her "twist" to this very traditional design element.

THERE IS NO WRONG WAY
TO MAKE THE BED

We spend about a quarter of our lives in bed, and our preferences for how our "nests" are arranged can be very personal. While some love sleeping under the weight of heavy covers, others can only relax with a light sheet on top of them. And while some prefer to be tucked in tight, feet bound by sheets with perfectly taut hospital corners, others need more freedom to move around in their sleep and like to let their legs dangle out from under an untucked duvet. For any and all of these preferences, there is a way to make the bed that will look great and remain conducive to a perfect night's slumber. That said, here are some of my favorite tips to help making the bed second nature.

Under Cover: How OCD are you about making your bed? If you like the bed to look clean and crisp, I recommend a blanket cover, which is less fussy than a duvet. If you like a really soft and tussled look, then you will love a soft and inviting duvet cover. If your mood changes, have both, and alternate depending on the season.

Folding the Duvet: Typically, if you are using the duvet cover folded at the foot, you should fold it in thirds. If the duvet cover has a monogram, you will need to fold in either end so that the monogram shows at the foot of the bed.

To Show or Not to Show: The top edge of the flat sheet (called the "turnback" or "foldback") is often embellished with a decorative edge, an inset border, or a monogram. These decorative elements may be put on display by folding the sheet over the blanket or duvet cover and limiting the number of pillows stacked at the head of the bed.

Pillow Talk: Sleeping pillows are typically stacked horizontally behind the decorative shams. If you sleep on a French case instead of a traditional case, you have the added benefit of using the same pillows for sleeping and decoration.

An elegant, Emeline scroll appliqué border in a handsome shade of caramel—the perfect accent to rich wallpaper and headboard patterns—in a room by Walker Simmons Designs.

As much as I love to work with colorful accents, white-on-white linens are the most traditional expression of elegance there is, and for that reason, this look remains a popular choice. Right: White-on-white embroidery is the most commonly found in vintage linens—why not reinvent this old standard for your modern sensibility? A simple line-and-dot motif is a contemporary interpretation. Above: Modern yet serene is the result in this room by Delphine Krakoff. The bed is simply constructed with all-white bedding, from the tucked-in blanket cover to the thin blanket veiling the foot. Opposite: In this room by Gerrie Bremermann, shade after shade of white are used to create an unexpectedly rich bed, from the crisp white fabric to the subtly shaded monogram that complements the duvet cover folded at the foot.

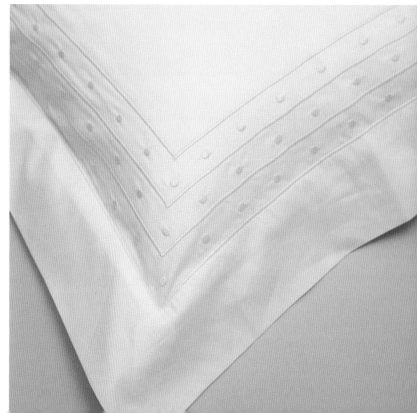

Blue-and-white linens are as popular today as the traditional all-white linens of the past. Blue is one of the most universally liked colors—its appeal no doubt due to its pure, calming quality. Top: Classic and sleek intermix in a chic bedroom by Eric Cohler, with a downy duvet softening the tucked-in blanket cover and large appliqué Greek key motif. Bottom: Cathy Kincaid Hudson layers row after row of pillows in the softest shades of blue for an exquisitely inviting bed. Opposite: Crisp, cool, and calming . . . vibrant white bedding is the perfect extension of the white furniture accents and soft blue walls in a room by designer Susan Palma.

PLAYING WITH PATTERN

I love mixing patterns for adding dimension and interest to a bed. Here are the ways I suggest working pattern in.

- Use a patterned fabric for the bed skirt or box spring cover. It's a great place to either mimic or complement a favorite fabric on the wall or drapes.

- A set of sheets with a sweet or subtle pattern hiding under a classic white blanket cover is a lovely visual treat for you, and only you, to enjoy as you peel back the bed each night.

- Copy or interpret a pattern from an upholstered piece in the room and put it on Euro shams. It's is a nice way to tie in the bed with the rest of the room.

- A little pattern goes a long way. For those timid about too much pattern, start with a pair of pillowcases.

Above: Charlotte Moss uses the same fabric throughout the room—down to the Euro shams and duvet cover—for a seamless play on pattern. Opposite: In my own bedroom, a beautiful floral-patterned sham by D. Porthault is the perfect tie-in with the embroidered trellis motif of the Euro shams and blanket cover. It's a charming backdrop for the sweetest of dreams.

MIXING PATTERNS WITH
PILLOWCASES

CATHY KINCAID HUDSON

If you want a room to make a statement, do it with pillow covers, which is one of the best ways, especially if your headboard is simple. I love to mix pillowcase patterns—some plain, some floral or even polka-dotted—as long as the colors coordinate. Antique textile pillows can add a softness to the bed and make it more interesting. Exotic textiles are also a wonderful layering element.

Neck rolls done in great color combinations—not necessarily to match the rest of the bed linens—are always the punch that makes the room.

In a room by Cathy Kincaid Hudson, pattern is used to striking effect. Cathy mixes different patterns on the wall, the drapes, the shams, and the blanket, tying it all together with a common color.

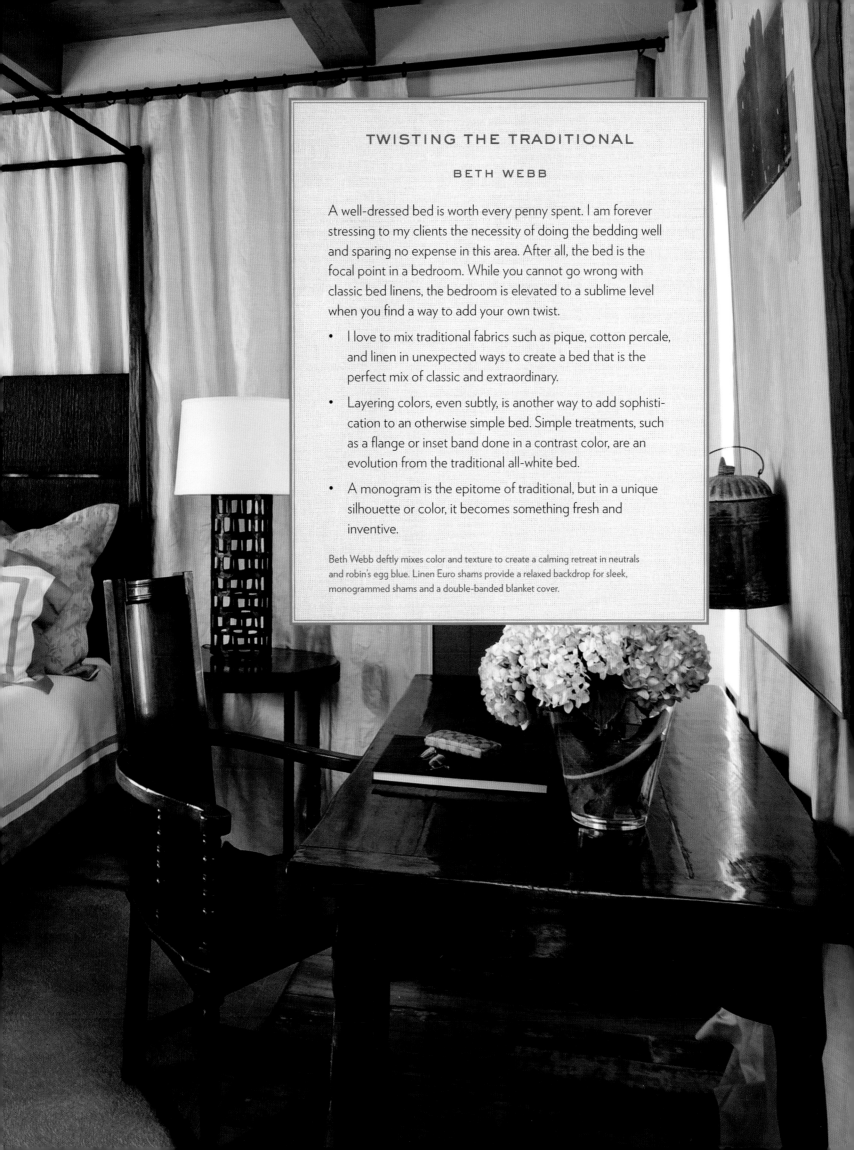

TWISTING THE TRADITIONAL

BETH WEBB

A well-dressed bed is worth every penny spent. I am forever stressing to my clients the necessity of doing the bedding well and sparing no expense in this area. After all, the bed is the focal point in a bedroom. While you cannot go wrong with classic bed linens, the bedroom is elevated to a sublime level when you find a way to add your own twist.

- I love to mix traditional fabrics such as pique, cotton percale, and linen in unexpected ways to create a bed that is the perfect mix of classic and extraordinary.

- Layering colors, even subtly, is another way to add sophistication to an otherwise simple bed. Simple treatments, such as a flange or inset band done in a contrast color, are an evolution from the traditional all-white bed.

- A monogram is the epitome of traditional, but in a unique silhouette or color, it becomes something fresh and inventive.

Beth Webb deftly mixes color and texture to create a calming retreat in neutrals and robin's egg blue. Linen Euro shams provide a relaxed backdrop for sleek, monogrammed shams and a double-banded blanket cover.

THE ICONOCLAST

A ZEAL FOR BOLD COLOR AND STYLE

 THE DICTIONARY defines an iconoclast as someone who challenges or over-turns custom and tradition. It sounds a little radical put that way, but the basic gist is that you're not big on rules — not inclined to follow the crowd or take the safe route. It takes guts and confidence to be an iconoclast, and if you embrace that path whenever you head out to greet the world, shouldn't your home welcome you back with the same kind of always-up-for-a-surprise personality?

As someone who loves doing things differently, you're better positioned than any-one to take the fullest advantage of what linens can do. You can play with pattern, tex-ture, and color in ways most would shy away from. Your environment is in joyful motion when you don't hold onto rules so tightly; you can mix and swap out and recombine and it will always work.

An orange chevron-quilted spread over sheets appliquéd in pink eyelet? Go for it. A black powder room with citron hand towels hanging from mismatched hooks? Great. An appliquéd Greek key border paired with an unexpected Suzani throw? It will trans-form your bedroom into a work of art.

Black walls and a banquette-style headboard frame a truly subversive bed by Eric Cohler. Clean white bedding accented with flaxen linen shams tie in with the neutral headboard, while a bold Suzani serves double duty as a duvet cover that complements the lamps.

EMBRACING COLOR

Fear not color! More than any other element of design, color reveals your personality in a vivid and universal language. Linens are the perfect way to infuse a room with color. Unlike wall coverings or draperies, bed linens are both collectible and noncommittal. In this sense, the bed is a quick-change artist, allowing you to change the entire look of your room seasonally—or even with your weekly laundry—to suit your mood.

And, by the way, who says colors have to match all the time? The term *colorful* also suggests fun. So have fun, and color outside the lines: Pair your sapphire blue quilt with orange-emblazoned shams, dress your bed in a bright red wool blanket cover, or layer it in the softest shades of lavender. Letting your true colors show in your bedroom is a simple and fun way to reveal your personality.

Previous pages, left: The interplay of
complementary shades of blue and green has
a serene effect in a room by Ruthie Sommers.
Previous pages, right: Color inspiration can
be found in the smallest of places. Here, the
persimmon shade of the elaborately oversized
appliquéd monogram ties in with the adjacent
artwork. The deep sapphire-hued quilt at the
foot of the bed adds further sophistication to
the room.

Above: Rich brown is no longer a neutral
in the elaborately patterned curtain or the
delicate embroidery on the French cases in a
room designed by Richard Keith Langham.
Opposite: The floral appliqué resonates with
this lavender bedroom by Andrew Raquet,
lending both serenity and sophistication.

DESIGNING WITH COLOR

KATIE RIDDER

Since the furnishings scheme of a bedroom revolves around the bed, linens are an important way to add color and enhance the design of the whole room. I prefer white or cream linens, which allow me to introduce color in borders and decorative motifs. My favorite places for color are on the leading edge of the top sheet and as frames on the pillowcase and duvet. Here, with a few small ribbons of color, I can reflect the feeling of the entire room. One trick I love is to use stitching in a contrasting color that's a nod to another piece in the room, such as a lampshade or a valence.

Color is the star in two rooms by Katie Ridder. Above: Katie uses custom linens not only to link the bed to the rest of her eclectic choices, but also to help ground the overall look. Bright orange appliquéd borders on the shams and a unique medallion trim on the sheets and pillowcases make this bed hold its own against the other striking patterns and colors at play in this chic bohemian bedroom. Opposite: Colors pulled from a spice market inform this bedroom full of exotic touches. The Chinese red blanket is the key linen piece, marrying the curry-colored bed and the bold wallpaper pattern.

COLORFUL BEDROOMS

RICHARD KEITH LANGHAM

I always tell my clients to spend lots of money on your shoes and your sheets—you are always in either one or the other!

Bed linens are the icing on the cake in any bedroom, and icing is tastier with a little color. I love to use pastel or ivory-colored cotton or linen sheets, punctuated with embroidery or appliqué in a bold color or contrasting flange. Luscious color turns the bed into an inviting oasis and provides a perfect finishing touch to any colorful room.

Richard Keith Langham uses opulence and plays with color to create the most heavenly of beds. Above, left: Soft shades of sage and peapod green create a tranquil alcove, while the pop of fuchsia hints at a more playful side. Above, right: Bathed in a rich coral, this bed is a sumptuously warm invitation to slumber. Opposite: Hand-dyed silk in shades of blue and green ensconce the bed in a dreamlike state.

Black and white is an inherently striking combination in two rooms by Melissa Rufty. Above: A charmingly detailed bolster, with its unique envelope closure, makes its own statement, but when piped in black, it creates the perfect tie-in to the Euro shams, blanket cover, and window treatment. Opposite: Graphic black-and-white pillows are in stark contrast to the warm coral palette of the room.

VERSATILE BEDDING

ALEX PAPACHRISTIDIS

It's very important that the bed be special and the focal point of the bedroom. I love a luxurious, fabulous, statement bed that draws you into the room.

I make a bed using matching fitted and top sheets, a duvet cover, and four pillows stacked on top of each other with two decorative shams in front. For the cover, I add a custom embroidered pattern on three sides, which forms a frame around the bed when the duvet is tucked in tightly. It's either classic or modern depending on the client and, of course, it references the colors in the room. Then I'll add two custom decorative pillows, which sit in front of the shams, made in fabrics used in other places in the room, or in fabrics that complement the room. It's good to use different patterns on the front and back, so the client can switch things around when they feel like a quick change.

At the foot of the bed, I like a batik bedspread, a fur throw, or a custom bedspread made from a fabric in the room, quilted on the back with another pattern so that the client has different options for different times of the year. Changing the bedspreads seasonally makes a room seem "redone."

Alex Papachristidis demonstrates how bedding can be used to transform a room. In both versions of this bedroom, you'll note the same headboard, sunburst mirror, miniature chair, and lamps. Yet with a change of palette to the wall and the bed linens, the two interiors could not look more different.

Above: Pattern and color work together to create
a casual yet no less sophisticated bed. A vintage-
inspired chenille blanket cover is home to a mix of
shams. The Euro shams unify the ensemble, and the
lemon-yellow monogrammed pillows are meant to
stand in pure contrast.

Opposite: A bed designed by Larry Laslo exclusively
in black and white reads as incredibly chic. The
monogram is an essential addition to the mix; without
it, the pillow would look blank against the strong
pattern of the spread and canopy.

BEDROOM COUTURE

Dressing oneself and dressing one's home should have little distinction for anyone with a passion for style and personal expression. So if you're a dyed-in-the-wool-crepe fashionista, your linen closet is going to reflect the same exuberance as the closet housing your collection of Manolos and Marc Jacobs.

The ability to change your clothing style on a whim, from gypset chic to Park Avenue polish, is what stimulates and inspires you, and a broad collection of custom linens allows you to do the same for your table, bedroom, and bath.

And just as seasonal changes introduce knits and leather into your wardrobe, your bedroom can turn from cool white linens with pastel accents to more substantial sheets bordered in intricate ring stitching and covered in a deep ocher satin quilt and a paisley cashmere throw in the colors of Indian spices.

Even those of you with the best eye sometimes walk out of a boutique with that piece you'll wear once and then retire to the back of the closet, wondering why you bought it. This is much less likely to happen with custom linens, no matter how boldly rendered the appliqué. After all, no one's going to raise an eyebrow at a bed wearing the same thing twice.

A bedroom as perfectly coordinated as a well-put-together outfit. The strokes of white, saturated colors, and rich detailing are apparent in the linens as much as in the rest of the décor. Design by Beth Webb.

Connecting your linen pieces and bedding
thematically with the other bedroom décor makes
for an easy "costume change" for the bed. A stack
of rich fabrics featuring jewel tones, embroidered
wool throws, and batik-patterned covers all intermix
with this rich ocher bedroom by Katie Ridder,
offering a fresh look that suits your mood.

THE FASHION OF FINE LINENS

LAURA VINROOT POOLE

Fashion is a form of expression in daily life. It communicates to the world who you are, where you come from, and where you are headed. Just as clothing tells the story of your persona outside the home, linens tell a more private tale. As with clothing, living with fine linens is not about money. It is about style, dignity, and self-respect. It is about the time and care involved in soaking a Sunday supper stain in lemon juice or the patience for pressing the perfect crease on a boudoir pillowcase. It is taking care to store linens carefully inside a cedar drawer and ensuring that you always have a clean handkerchief in your pocketbook. Fine linens are the inward expression of our family's heritage and the most private and intimate expression of our personal identity.

With pretty light filtering through its enormous windows, this master bedroom designed by Gwen Driscoll is at once elegant, classic, and refined—the epitome of timeless fashion.

STYLE SENSE

MARK BADGLEY & JAMES MISCHKA

JM: Our style harks back to the glamorous Hollywood of the for-ties. The Badgley Mischka signature look is simple, streamlined, and thoroughly elegant; at the same time, there is always an element of extravagance. Our philosophy of fashion in clothing is not too different from our philosophy of dressing the bed. "Sleek and elegant" is an apt description of the master bed in our country home—white with black trim, clean lines, and the simplest of monogram letter style.

MB: Classic style is hard to come by in fashion for both women and the home. That's why we all crave it. We believe a woman should feel glam-orous and comfortable in a beautiful gown, and that she should feel all the more so when climbing into her bed at the end of the day. Fashion and interiors both can be over-the-top; the trick is where to pull back to let classic design principles rule. Of course, a little bit of indulgence is always welcome, and there is no place to better enjoy being "fancy" than in your own bed.

Bold, modern letterforms stamped across linen French cases take the traditional monogrammed pillow past the ordinary and telecast "custom" as strongly as the rest of the masculine design pieces in this bedroom.

Above: Liz Caan mixes both classic and unexpected elements in a master bedroom. Bold, orange appliquéd shams and a fur throw work together to create a room that is at once inviting and fun. Opposite: An unusual interplay of textures has dramatic effect in a master bedroom designed by Delphine Krakoff. Classic percale is mixed with a faux-fur cover for a layering of tactile experiences. Following Pages: This intensely hued wallpaper calls for linen details that calm the bold décor. Classic and exotic architectural elements such as the quatrefoil-shaped monogram and the exotic silhouette of the headboard pleasantly contradict each other, while a classic toile pattern is made matchless in eye-popping color. Design by MMR Interiors.

THE HEDONIST

FULLY IMMERSED IN BATH LINENS

IN THE FABLE "The Ant and the Grasshopper," the grasshopper is cast as a hedonist because he prefers to spend his days enjoying the comforts of life as opposed to working day and night until his thorax is aching. While we humans are not so easily summed up, it wouldn't be terrible for more of us to embrace the hedonist's ethos. Work is important, of course, but downtime is just as crucial, and nestling into a bathroom outfitted in thick terry and cottons that rival your softest bedding is the best way to settle down.

You can fill your linen closet with the plushest of Egyptian cotton terry, indulgently embellished with ornate borders or breezy tassels and marked with your monogram. If you line the cold marble floor of your bathroom with quilted terry mats, your own feet are as indulged as the rest of you. And no mere towels for you, hedonist. Your preference runs toward the decadence of a bath sheet, dramatically sized to envelop you completely in its generous embrace, and you keep enough of them stocked so that you never have to use the same towel twice in a row. A fresh towel after every bath or shower is the definition of indulgence.

Celebratory cocktails with friends? Sure, count you in, but nothing closes a successful day like sinking into a hot bath with a pint of Ben & Jerry's, knowing that when you're finally ready to emerge, the fluffiest towel awaits your warm skin, followed by a robe of cooling pique with your monogram on the pocket. By the time you don your silk pj's and slide into your fine linen sheets, the satisfaction of making the most out of both business and pleasure eases you into sleep.

A neat stack of towels placed bath-side awaits your reluctant return to the real world.

Above: The old-fashioned touch of this wooden stand against classic white tiles calls for towels with a similar nod to tradition, in this case a charming laurel pattern around a monogram. Design by Leigh Taylor Bornitz.
Opposite: Simple embellishments, such as piping in a cheerful color, make bath towels worthy of display, even when hung to dry.

When you love indulgent bathrooms, why stop
at the towels? They are just as important to the
experience as the tub and faucets, and deserve
the same attention to detail. Above: Scalloped
edging, rich earth-tone embroidery, and a two-tone
monogram make these towels special. Opposite:
This indulgent bath alcove by Suzanne Kasler
wouldn't be quite as luxurious without towels as
elegant as the other details.

TOWEL RECOMMENDATIONS AND TIPS ON SELECTING TERRY

Indulgent comfort is as important in the bath as it is in the bedroom, but when it comes to the bath, form absolutely must follow function. Here are a few tips to ensure that your towels are not only beautiful but practical.

The Beauty of Simplicity: Though piping gives a great finished look to washcloths, I don't recommend monogramming or otherwise embellishing them. Washcloths are utilitarian, and nobody wants to scrub their face with a monogram.

Terry in the Powder Room: We've all walked into the powder room at a party, washed our hands, and realized with dread that the only option for drying is an impeccably pressed linen guest towel. Nobody wants to "ruin" the fine linens on display, and so we end up drying our hands with our clothing or waving them around like a crazy person. My cure for this predicament is to have a stack of terry fingertip towels placed at the washbasin as a less intimidating option for guests.

The Quilted Mat: Unlike your typical bath rug, the quilted mat is made to measure for a space of any size, from the most miniscule of Manhattan bathrooms to the grandest of Texas tubs. Not to mention, it can be tossed into the wash with its matching towels on a regular basis. The quilted mat, two plush pieces of terry quilted together, is the perfect alternative to those department-store bathmats.

Terry's Aging Properties and the Importance of Quality and Rotation: Even the best terry cloth is going to degrade faster than a fine linen or cotton weave. Don't let it bother you. Instead, focus on rotation. The more towels you have in your closet, the longer they will last. Not to mention, you'll enjoy the fresh look of a different set.

Left: Playful fingertips by D. Porthault are paired with the Chopstick style monogram for a perfect complement to the colorful Chinoiserie wallpaper by Meg Braff. Opposite (clockwise from top, left): A monogram in a strong green pairs well with the wood-slab vanity; For an eclectic look, layer different sizes, border treatments, colors and even a mix of monogram styles; Your feet will thank you every time you step onto a custom terry mat in a marble bathroom; A Greek key trim in pale blue is a perfect accent to this simple white vessel sink; Towels that reference a pattern and color in your shower curtain are a sure way to say "custom" in the bath.

Above: Trimming the towels in an assortment of colors
creates a charming palette.
Opposite: A bathroom by Katie Ridder shows a casual
option for storing towels by rolling them in a basket.

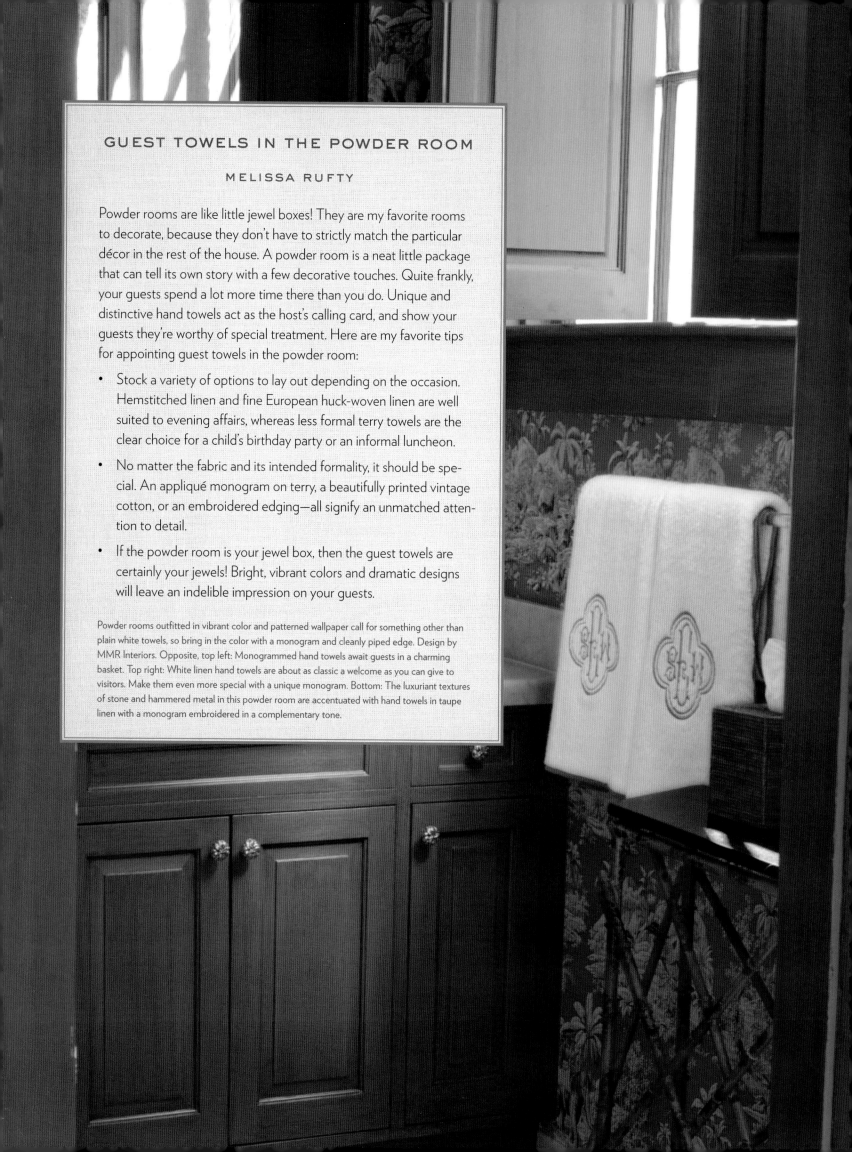

GUEST TOWELS IN THE POWDER ROOM

MELISSA RUFTY

Powder rooms are like little jewel boxes! They are my favorite rooms to decorate, because they don't have to strictly match the particular décor in the rest of the house. A powder room is a neat little package that can tell its own story with a few decorative touches. Quite frankly, your guests spend a lot more time there than you do. Unique and distinctive hand towels act as the host's calling card, and show your guests they're worthy of special treatment. Here are my favorite tips for appointing guest towels in the powder room:

- Stock a variety of options to lay out depending on the occasion. Hemstitched linen and fine European huck-woven linen are well suited to evening affairs, whereas less formal terry towels are the clear choice for a child's birthday party or an informal luncheon.

- No matter the fabric and its intended formality, it should be special. An appliqué monogram on terry, a beautifully printed vintage cotton, or an embroidered edging—all signify an unmatched attention to detail.

- If the powder room is your jewel box, then the guest towels are certainly your jewels! Bright, vibrant colors and dramatic designs will leave an indelible impression on your guests.

Powder rooms outfitted in vibrant color and patterned wallpaper call for something other than plain white towels, so bring in the color with a monogram and cleanly piped edge. Design by MMR Interiors. Opposite, top left: Monogrammed hand towels await guests in a charming basket. Top right: White linen hand towels are about as classic a welcome as you can give to visitors. Make them even more special with a unique monogram. Bottom: The luxuriant textures of stone and hammered metal in this powder room are accentuated with hand towels in taupe linen with a monogram embroidered in a complementary tone.

LUXURIOUS BATHROOMS

MELISSA RUFTY

The bathroom is usually the first room you see in the morning and the last room you see before going to bed. It is where you should treat yourself to every indulgence. I like to think of it as a personal spa, without the intrusion of attendants. Accordingly, I outfit my bathroom as if it were in a luxury resort. This means stocking it with exquisite custom towels, a plush robe, and bath-mats, all of which are personalized in some way, whether with a trim in a favorite color or a monogram. Scented candles, soaps in glass terrines, and my go-to fragrance finish off the indulgent experience, and create a space that truly reflects my penchant for indulgent spaces.

Below: When you call attention to hand towels by arranging them in a basket, they need to stand up to the scrutiny. A bold appliquéd monogram does the trick in a powder room by Charlotte Moss. Opposite: The mix of patterns in this beautifully detailed bathroom transports you to an exotic Moroccan resort. This calls for towels that echo the sentiment. A geometric monogram in a soft teal references the color and shape of the tiles as well as the inlay on the cabinet. Design by Cathy Kincaid Hudson. Following pages: The possibilities are endless when selecting a color in which to trim towels. Binding the towels is not only decorative, but it also adds to the life of the towel, protecting the edges from normal wear and tear.

THE EVERYDAY ENTERTAINER

FINE LINENS FOR EVERYDAY EVENTS

 HOME IS WHERE THE HEART IS. Your fondest, most intimate memories are born within the walls of your home. They accumulate in the most mundane places and tie themselves to the everyday rituals that you create with your family and close friends. There is a fine art to infusing one's home with the endearing details that will become your fondest memories. As a home-maker, your focus is inward, making the most private parts of your family's day memorable and special.

Infusing your daily rituals with the added luxury of even the simplest of fine linens plants a seed within your children that will grow for a lifetime. A rushed breakfast, counting down the minutes until the school bus turns into the driveway, is no less chaotic with a printed cotton napkin, but as you clean the table, there is a certain comfort in tossing that napkin into the hamper instead of the trash can. Using your silver tea service along with primly monogrammed lunch napkins makes an ordinary visit with your dearest friend something extraordinary. Playing a parlor game with a glass of sherry or an evening cocktail nestled in a vintage cocktail napkin becomes a cherished memory.

The special touches that fine linens add to the everyday events taking place in the kitchen, the den, the porch—these are the memories that leave an indelible mark in the minds of your friends, family, and houseguests, and that make your home one of the fond-est places in their collective memory bank.

Make the everyday extraordinary with a few simple touches and some ingenuity. Take a cue from your classic wardrobe and allow your Hermès scarf to be the backdrop to a well-dressed table setting. With a little luck, you'll have a monogrammed napkin in the perfect shade to make something thrown together look completely purposeful.

Above, left: A simple breakfast in bed: A pin-tucked napkin is used as an impromptu placemat and paired with a napkin detailed simply with an appliqué horsebit motif. Above, right and opposite: A leisurely weekend breakfast at the kitchen table can be elegant in its simplicity. Quilted cotton placemats and charming block-printed napkins in bright and opposing hues are easy touches.

Above: An indulgent afternoon treat of delicate French macaroons and ladyfingers are served on classic white linens. Opposite: A traditional tea service is made all the more engaging with monogrammed tea napkins.

CONTRASTING
UPTOWN AND DOWNTOWN

The idea of mixing high and low can often send the decoratively timid running for their "white on white." But really it is not that hard to conjure the sophistication and energy that uptown/downtown scenarios create. Try one of these pairings for an eclectic tablescape:

• Rattan placemats with monogrammed napkins

• A batik tablecloth with white hemstitched napkins and your fine china

• Melamine plates on a crisp white tablecloth

• Mismatched linens, china, and silverware

• Seersucker napkins under cocktails in vintage glassware

• A unique rope or ribbon in place of napkin rings

An Indian block-print cotton tablecloth, raffia placemats with a faux-hemstitch detail, and a casual linen napkin marked with an intricate monogram are a chic mix of high and low.

With a little imagination, any room can be the
dining room. A fireside dinner for two in the library,
mixing occasional chairs and an antique side
table with a voile scarf and elegant embroidered
dinner napkins, creates an intimate backdrop for a
memorable evening.

THE COCKTAIL NAPKIN

We all adore a good cocktail—and why shouldn't we? From watching an expert mixologist work his magic over a cocktail shaker to the spell cast by beautiful potions in gorgeous glasses of all shapes and sizes, there's nothing like a perfectly crafted cocktail to embody our joie de vivre.

What better way to deliver that drink to your guest than with a charming, beautiful cocktail napkin tucked under the glass? Cocktail napkins, unlike their more formal counterparts, are jovial in nature and are fun to collect in a variety of prints, colors, and monograms. I have dozens and dozens, some vintage, some cheeky, some extravagant—and find them an absolute necessity for any blossoming hostess. I prefer a rectangular shape (typically, six by eight inches), which allows for a monogram or decorative detail while still providing enough room to rest my drink above the design. Keep in mind, a drawer full of cocktail napkins will add that extra touch when you pass a drink to a friend in your home, signaling special attention from you the hostess!

AFTER the HUNT LOUISIANA'S AUTHORITATIVE COLLECTION OF WILD GAME & GAME FISH COOKERY

CHEF JOHN D. FOLSE, CEC, AAC

HORSES   MICHAEL EASTMAN   KNOPF

Take to the gentleman's study for a glass of port. Linen cocktail napkins with a chopstick-inspired monogram demonstrate that a monogram can be anything but traditional.

Top, bottom, and opposite: Charming vintage appliquéd cocktail napkins, available in a wide array of designs, are playful additions to a modern cocktail tray.

Following pages: Cocktail napkins are incredibly versatile and collectible, and an accessible way to entertain with fine linens. Left: Lavender seersucker cocktail squares with an embroidered seahorse detail playfully tie in with vintage aqua milk-glass goblets. Top right: Bright blue cocktail napkins feature an art deco–style embroidered monogram. Bottom right: Cocktail napkins in citron linen are accented with a masculine embroidered monogram.

COCKTAIL

I instinctively pull from my collection of cocktail napkins for all manner of occasions. From left to right: Vintage cocktail napkins featuring delicate embroidered flowers are a pretty choice for sherry at the bridge table; A prominent cipher monogram marks classic hemstitched linen; Charming pheasants in a nest are perfect for an afternoon parlor snack; A swinging monkey is a playful reminder to find the fun in everyday entertaining.

What's a proper parlor game without a cocktail? Above: Printed cocktail napkins paired with mint juleps are the perfect accompaniment to a quiet game of backgammon. Opposite: Your friends' poker faces will melt away with a serving or two of scotch, elegantly presented on a monogrammed cocktail napkin.

Above and opposite: Cocktail napkins are integral to a well-stocked bar. Crisp, white hemstitched linen is embroidered with the Dorea monogram style—a cipher design with intricate hand-embroidered seed stitching in a deep shade of espresso to complement the bar's dark wood.

MEASURING FOR THE TABLECLOTH SIZE AND SHAPE

Tablecloths make great decorative statements, but they are also practical, offering protection to fine wood finishes and providing insulation to reduce noise. But with dining tables available in such a wide variety of shapes and sizes, it is nearly impossible to find a ready-made tablecloth that fits exactly right. So here are some pointers to getting that perfect Renaissance-painting drape.

Round Tables: Round cloths are typically used on round tables and are usually floor-length. You can lay a square "topper" cloth over them for a layered look. To measure a round table, you need the widest diameter, which means making sure that the tape measure crosses the center point of the table. In other words, it will be the widest measurement you can achieve running the tape measure from one side to the other.

Racetrack Tables: When you add leaves to a round table, you get a racetrack shape. An oblong (rectangular) cloth will be the correct fit here. When laid, it will be longer at the corners than the sides. You can order the oblong cloth with

rounded corners to prevent "spires" in the corners. Measuring a racetrack requires determining the length from center to center of each curved end (the widest point) as well as the width from edge to edge across the narrower part.

Square and Rectangular Tables: For square tables, a square tablecloth is the appropriate shape. For rectangular tables, an oblong cloth works best. Simply measure both the length and width to determine your tabletop size.

Oval Tables: You can use an oblong tablecloth on an oval table, but be advised that the tablecloth will spire dramatically in the corners and may touch the floor. A custom oval tablecloth must be ordered if you want a uniform drop along the table's edge. Measure oval tables across the two widest points, both lengthwise and widthwise.

Calculating Drop: The drop or overhang is the distance between the top of the table and the hem of the tablecloth. The average dining table is twenty-seven to thirty inches high, and most dining chairs are sixteen inches from the floor. In most cases, the recommendation is that the hem of the tablecloth graze the seat of the dining chair, which typically equals a drop of ten to twelve inches. Floor-length tablecloths are not as common at a dining table but are often ordered for a side table or buffet table. When ordering a floor-length tablecloth, measure from the top of the table to the floor. For a floor-length tablecloth, I recommend rounded corners to prevent "puddling" in the corners.

Left: Accomplish the perfect length for your tablecloth by measuring with a soft tape measure. Opposite: A classic hemstitched linen tablecloth is a basic necessity for any dining room. Paired with matching napkins, it echoes the most traditional of settings.

OUTDOOR ENTERTAINING

AMANDA LINDROTH

Linens have been a personal fascination of mine since I was in my early twenties—from the basic, scalloped cotton sheets of my childhood to a journey through various extravagances and wonderful vintage finds since then. Good linens are dreamy, romantic, and necessary.

I live in the Islands, where we are deprived of shopping and lots of other conveniences but spoiled by a magical, breezy, old-fashioned lifestyle. We live with the doors open year-round. We dine by candlelight (sometimes because the power is out!), and our tables are dressed with shells from the sea and leaves and flowers from the garden. Bougainvillea, yes; peonies, no . . . our aesthetic is driven by what is available in our front yards and on the beach.

I have drawers and drawers of favorite napkins. Some of them are giant, thirty-inch square, damask, English and French, and initialed (someone else's). Other favorites include vintage, hand-embroidered "Nassau" lunch napkins from the fifties. They were a lucky score from an old estate here. I am not at all snobby about provenance. My most recent purchase was thirty-six beautiful cotton batik napkins from a local hardware store. They are simply perfect! I am compulsive about buying linens and shop constantly for them on eBay, at antique shows and shops, and through dealers.

For parties, I have sixty vintage pink lunch napkins that make their way to tables laid with antique raspberry-colored Herend dishes and mountains of pink bougainvillea piled up as centerpieces. I like to add Messel-colored wineglasses to those pink tables. The result is a fresh, island-y, happy veranda.

Our eight-year-old eats with a cloth napkin at every meal. Spaghetti Bolognese has wreaked a fair amount of havoc, but paper napkins are out of the question!

Move outside for ambiance only Mother Nature can provide. Here, a tablecloth with an elaborately appliquéd cane pattern creates a peaceful setting for an intimate dinner with friends.

Vintage lapkins laid over the back of each chair warmly welcome your guests to the table. Following pages: A beautiful monogram in a shade of rich goldenrod pulled from the tablecloth is the focal point of this neutral place setting.

NAPKINS, LAPKINS, AND PLENTY OF THEM

SUZANNE RHEINSTEIN

I do have an abundance of linens for the table—or the lap! My husband and I love to feed our friends and their friends, often at big buffets with everyone eating all over the house and garden. So I have collected stacks and stacks of generous old French linen damask napkins, which I buy whenever I am at the Marché au Puces in France or from Lucullus in New Orleans, Patrick Dunne's ode to all things beautiful for the table. One of the best parts about these old napkins is the hand-embroidered monograms in the middle, most of them elaborate and perhaps worked by the ladies of the house. Some linens I have because they are too beautifully made to let them settle into oblivion. I am thinking of some of the gorgeous Marghab linens. The ones I have with tiny strawberries are a bit too sweet for me, yet the embroidery is so well done I had to save them!

THE SOCIAL BUTTERFLY

ENTERTAINING WITH TABLE LINENS

YOU'RE A PEOPLE PERSON. While others are lamenting the loss of privacy, you're setting a table for twenty. As the host with the most, nothing is more important than showing your friends and family—and anyone else who drops by—the best time they can possibly have. And because entertaining just doesn't work as well or go as smoothly without the right setting, a plentiful and varied collection of linens is essential.

Linens are the way to put your signature on large-scale gatherings. My suggestion? Think colors, textures, sizes. Have enough to multiply your options. Something as seemingly innocuous as a napkin will signal to what extent you go to provide a good time . . . a cocktail held aloft with a bright little square of green, a generous swath of navy-monogrammed white on a lap, tables around a pool skirted in cocoa linen with fretwork borders. A grouping of serving pieces that shows your innate knowledge of etiquette won't come off without a design scheme to your linens that displays real hosting imagination and a desire to make your guests as comfortable and stimulated as possible. It's the bountiful, elegant, and indulgent tablescape that makes the event truly yours. It shows you care about the smallest detail, and though your delightful pattern-mixing at a mixer may not get as much airtime as the politics no one's supposed to talk about yet always does, believe me, guests are drinking in the atmosphere your accoutrement sets as heartily as they are your wine.

Create a night to remember with the elegance that only fine linens can provide.

THE LBD OF TABLE SETTING: IVORY & GOLD

The perfect Little Black Dress (LBD), accessorized minimally, makes for an effortless yet effective evening. The equivalent of this idea in terms of a dinner party are ivory linens with a muted gold monogram. It's an incredibly versatile combination that skirts classic and modern, and is unstudied yet polished. If you have the room or budget for only one set of linens for entertaining, you'll be best served by this tested combination.

Soft and warm, ivory hemstitched linen embellished with a classically ornate monogram in muted gold is my most versatile table setting.

CREATING MEMORABLE DINNER PARTIES

FRANCES SCHULTZ

Nothing dresses up a table like beautiful linens. One of the most attainable routes to creating a sense of occasion is to set a beautiful table, however simple or grand. A sense of occasion heightens our awareness of the moment; it calls us to be present. If we can get a little bit of that with a centerpiece and good napkins—and we can—it is all to the good.

- Plain or fancy, a setting with lovely linens is a love note to all who are joining you at the table.

- If you are having a dinner party, it is good to have the table a *little* crowded. It's more intimate and usually more fun. You might opt for a sixty-inch round instead of a seventy-inch. If the table is rectangular, a thirty-inch width is easy to talk across.

- As for the tablescape itself . . . for all you picture takers out there, the fuller, the better. Bare spots on dining tables do not photograph well.

- Elsewhere in the dining room, I can't think of anything more elegant than monogrammed linen slipcovers or antimacassars for dining chairs.

- Have a seating plan, however orchestrated. It can be scribbled on the back of an envelope, or more formally presented and accompanied by place cards, but have a plan. It eliminates the awkwardness of choosing one's own position and allows the hostess to balance the shy with the talker, the prim with the naughty. I usually have some version of the plan on display, be it on an embossed leather board on an easel or a handwritten version clipped to the branch of a plant. Call guests' attention to it if they do not see it. Otherwise, they will spend the entire drinks hour (unwittingly) talking to their dinner partner because *this is just what happens*. It is a law of the universe. A seating plan also heightens the sense of occasion, which is the point.

Previous pages and left: A warm invitation to dine, with the backdrop of spring, inspires an interplay of colorful linens, china, and flowers. Following pages: An outdoor event has an air of casual elegance when placemats of butcher paper are paired with appliquéd dinner napkins knotted with a heavy rope.

THE SQUARE PLACEMAT

A square placemat is a wonderful alternative to the more common, oblong silhouette for many reasons:

- On a round table, square mats allow you to fit more settings gracefully.

- The square mats act as chargers of sorts, framing the china and allowing more room to display linen napkins, beautifully arranged in napkin rings, atop the plates.

- The square shape allows for more of your beautiful dining room table to show through the set table, making the rich wood a more prominent component of the tablescape.

- Square mats create a more intimate, fun, and informal table, which can be set closer together for a crowded, jovial grouping of friends.

A square placemat in teal linen is embellished with a bright pink monogram to create a delightful tablescape.

Custom embroidery allows you to perfectly match the colors of your fine china pattern. Here, crisp white linen is accented in shades of navy and rust to create a place setting that is impeccably coordinated.

Opposite: Nathan Turner sets the stage for an elegant evening with a beautiful blue paisley-inspired block-print cloth and crisp white dinner napkins with a blue monogram.

TABLESCAPES

NATHAN TURNER

I used to love to help my mother set the table for her dinner parties. Everything was much finer than what we used every day, especially the antique linens, with their intricate embroidery and decoration.

So it's no wonder I still like to set a table with good, embroidered linens. What I learned from my very social mom is that when you entertain, a lot of thought and care goes into what you serve—and what sits under and alongside that meal has to be up to the same standards. Customized linens show a concern for quality in every aspect of the meal. They also add textural interest and personalize the table.

I especially like to mix and match vintage linens, or use very fine embroidered linens on a more casual table.

Two interpretations of elegance—the same table takes on a split personality when dressed in drastically different styles. Above: A batik tablecloth in warm jewel tones is accented with a turquoise version of the Addison monogram. Opposite: In contrast, simple white linen creates an air of the traditional.

DRESSING THE TABLE WITH COLOR

The art of gracious entertaining lies in creating different experiences for your guests. I find that the more I entertain, the more I try to create a mood and ambience for my guests. Nothing is more versatile when creating an inviting table than an array of colorful linens.

- Colorful linens welcome your guests and set them at ease, as opposed to traditional white linens, which create an air of formality. Formality has its place; it's just not normally under the warmth of candlelight in my dining room!

- Having an assortment of linens in unexpected color combinations—rich aubergine accented in coral, a candy pink monogram on muted turquoise, a bright orange appliqué on soft brown—is the key to providing a dramatically different setting for each event.

- Eclectic colors are more versatile than you realize. It's amazing how suddenly the hydrangea you thought were white now echo a tinge of the lavender monogram on the table.

- Nothing demonstrates your sophistication as a hostess as much as richly layered colors on the table. The china and linens become playful companions, while the glassware and silver help to reflect and tie the entire tablescape together.

Opposite and following pages: Much like a brightly colored handbag, unique linens are just as adaptable as more traditional options. Here, an eggplant placemat is appliquéd with a border of coral and paired with a "chopstick" monogram for an unforgettable table bathed in color.

THE NEAT FREAK

LINEN CARE, STORAGE, AND INVENTORY

THOSE WITH A PROPENSITY FOR TIDINESS are sometimes called Type A. If your tendency is to take this as a slight, just ignore those who mock your focus on fastidiousness all the way to your envious armoire.

What you know is that life is always going to throw curveballs, so keeping those aspects of the day-to-day we *can* control under control puts you always one step ahead of the game.

The kind of organization and order that helps you breeze through your days with style and ease takes more than will. It takes skill. And ingenuity. Say an out-of-town friend suddenly finds herself stranded when her hotel overbooks. In no time, you've got a guest bedroom fitted out with crisp linen sheets, pillows in a variety of sizes and support, quilts and cashmere throws. Accommodations to rival the five-star room she was expecting.

Or your spouse calls, just after you've hosted an al fresco luncheon, to announce he's bringing an important client for dinner. A quick tuck into your beautifully-appointed linen armoire and you can set up an elegant ivory-and-gold table scenario with plenty of time left to raise a soufflé.

"Neat" has a lot of connotations. It defines not just how you behave, but who you are—simple, effective, and elegant. Keeping the accoutrements of the good life well-kept will not only make it easier for you to keep your cool, but will help your precious pieces stay pristine through the years, so in case your children inherit that Type A propensity, they'll appreciate the effort you took to keep their beautiful heirlooms in top condition.

An antique armoire houses perfectly arranged
bedroom linens.

LINEN INVENTORY

The guidelines for a proper linen inventory have changed a bit since the trousseau was first popularized centuries ago, but there remain basics that should form the core of your collection for daily use as well as special occasions:

MASTER BEDROOM

- 2 sets of sheets (flat, fitted, and pillowcases)
- 2 blanket covers (styled for summer and winter)
- 2 sets of shams to match the blanket covers
- 1 year-round blanket
- 1 duvet cover
- 1 throw quilt
- 2 his and hers wedge pillows for reading
- 2 boudoir or neck roll shams

MASTER BATHROOM

- 6 bath sheets
- 12 bath towels
- 12 hand towels
- 12 fingertip towels
- 12 washcloths
- 2 bath mats

GUEST BEDROOM

- 2 sets of sheets (flat, fitted, and pillowcases)
- 2 blanket covers (styled for summer and winter)
- 2 sets of shams to match the blanket covers
- 1 duvet cover
- 1 throw quilt
- 1 boudoir pillow or neck roll

GUEST BATHROOM

- 4 linen guest towels
- 4 bath sheets
- 6 bath towels
- 6 hand towels
- 6 fingertip towels
- 6 washcloths
- 2 bath mat

TABLETOP

- 1 casual tablecloth
- 1 formal tablecloth
- 6 linen guest towels
- 12 casual placemats and dinner napkins
- 12 formal placemats and dinner napkins
- 24 cocktail napkins

Even in detail, custom hand-embroidery is unmatched in its level of perfection. Fine cotton sheet sets, pique coverlets, and linen shams are all flawlessly stacked to showcase a variety of intricate embroidery styles.

LINEN CARE

- Using the coldest of water settings and lowest of dryer settings will ensure the long life of your linens. After all, there's a reason that antique and vintage linens are available, and it has a lot to do with hand washing and line drying! That's certainly not a practical approach as you look at the mounds of laundry that seem to appear overnight in the laundry hamper. So, my general rule for all laundry is this: machine wash warm, tumble dry low.

- Do not fear the laundry room! Fine linens get better with use; cottons and linens soften and take on a velveteen nature.

- Soaps: I recommend very gentle soaps, free of perfumes and dyes. Harsh detergents can break down the fibers with prolonged use and age the linens quickly.

- Any product that claims a bleaching property (whether it's chlorine based or oxygenated) is too harsh, even if it claims to be color safe and gentle. Chlorine, over time, will actually turn whites to their natural greige state—most people don't realize that white is a dyed color in natural fabrics.

- Do not overdry the linens—dry heat is more damaging to linens than any other element, because it breaks down the fibers. While it may take longer, I recommend the lowest temperature settings. Line drying, while not always practical, is the best way to ensure that your linens will last for generations.

- Iron the reverse side of the fabric to preserve any appliqué or embroidered details and to prevent shiny "scuff marks" on its face.

Left: For the neat freak, the laundry room is as well-appointed as any other room in the house. Opposite: Handwashing antique linens is the best way to prolong their life and ensure their continued place in your collection.

Above: Linens—freshly laundered and pressed—are stacked in the laundry basket and await their return to the linen closet. Opposite: There is nothing like climbing into a bed dressed with freshly pressed linens.

BEAUTIFUL LINENS DESERVE
BEAUTIFUL STORAGE

CHAROLOTTE MOSS

Unequivocally, one can never have enough linen storage. It seemed I was always poaching space from a cabinet here, a commode there, even though I had a linen closet. When I decided it was time to renovate the kitchen in East Hampton, the first thing that had to be worked into the plan? Linen storage. The Viking range would have to stand in line.

I am a visual person, therefore, I had to find a way to see my linens. Why, you ask. Because I take a great deal of time selecting and designing them, hunting down great antique napkins, waiting for some to be made, and taking the time to see that they are maintained. Everyone has a system that works for them, I guess. I had to find the right one for me. So, a wall of glass-front drawers was conceived and built for placemats and napkins. Tablecloths have their own location and system. A pullout shelf, about waist height, creates a workspace while I pull candidates from drawers, to create table settings, together with china, place cards, and the like.

Years ago, while working on a project in Tulsa, I met a woman named Keiki Jordan, who changed my ideas on storage forever. Never had I seen such beautiful drawers, or armoire and closet shelves. One of the simplest but most useful things she has done for me is to make quilted fabric–covered boards the size of a placemat to separate each set.

Sounds like a no-brainer, I know, but when you use the fabric you want, it makes storage another part of decorating—not just another mundane household task.

All I can say is that when I walk by my linen drawers and glance through the glass and everything looks pristine, I am resolved to start all kitchen designs right here with the linen storage, of course. The simplest, and most useful things can be beautiful, too.

Opposite and following pages: Charlotte Moss's impeccable linen closet allows for not only perfect organization, but also beautiful display. Glass allows for easy viewing of the linens inside each drawer, neatly stacked and arranged by color.

LINEN STORAGE

- After folding the sheet set, take a single pillow-case from the set, wrap it around the bundle, and face it out on the shelf so that you can easily identify the set.

- Do not starch your items before storing them, as the starch can yellow the fabric. It is best to store linens freshly laundered, and to press them before use.

- Certain woods can cause yellowing. Take care to protect linens when storing them in unlined trunks or armoires.

- Linens need fresh air to prevent yellowing, mildew, and dry rot. Do not store them in sealed plastic.

- Natural light will lead to fading and bleaching over time. Do not store linens where they are exposed to sunlight.

- Large tablecloths, especially linen ones, are often easier to store on long rolls, because creases are very difficult to iron out.

- Organize your napkins and placemats in stacks neatly tied to fabric-covered boards for easy organization and quick access.

PREPPING FOR THE PARTY

MARY MCDONALD

A big tip is to just always have everything starched and ironed ahead of the game. I like to tie each separate linen group together with grosgrain ribbons so you may easily lift and rummage around, pulling together your latest theme without single napkins or guest towels getting lost in unruly stacks falling all over. You can simply pull out the groups you like and all the remaining stays together in more easily manageable stacks, besides it looks pretty. Definitely plan your entire table whether buffet or sit down the day before and pull everything out to see what works and what doesn't. Being a perpetual collector of various themes I really need to pull out what my latest mix-and-match idea might be to see how much of one thing I have collected and how much of a festive impact it will have on a table (or not).

Dinner napkins, pressed and uniformly folded, are grouped by style and tied with ribbon to a fabric-covered board, an idea inspired by Charlotte Moss.

PLANNING IS EVERYTHING

The event is always a special one when you use your most beloved pieces. Along with fine china, your grandmother's silver, and the most delicate crystal, beautiful linens will show your guests that you had them in mind. Keeping these items at the ready is an important part of knowing what you have and not forgetting about things that haven't been used in a while.

In the days before an event, when the menu has been selected, it's time to start dreaming up the mood you want to set for your dinner guests. Search your closet or armoire for the linens, china, silverware, and other decorative accents that will set the stage for your evening. I recommend organizing your table linens in stacks neatly tied to fabric-covered boards for easy organization and quick access. Sort through your silver, and polish a piece or two if necessary. As for cocktail napkins, I recommend having on hand at least double the number of guests. Pull out your glassware and check it for dust or water marks. By laying everything out on the table, you can visualize the final setting and make choices for decorative touches such as candles and flowers.

Opposite: Table linens are housed in an antique armoire for easy review when planning the tablescape. Following pages: The stage is set: All the elements for an elegant dinner table are laid out and await being thoughtfully arranged.

PLACE SETTING GUIDE

BANQUET OR BRUNCH

BREAKFAST

LUNCH

DINNER

EUROPEAN

FORMAL

MONOGRAM ETIQUETTE

SINGLE INITIAL
A single initial can represent either the first or last name. Single initials are a nice option for a guest room or for informal table linens. Example: Mary Smith, Thomas Moore

THREE-LETTER MONOGRAM —STRAIGHT ACROSS
A three letter monogram is designed for an individual's name and is not suited for couples who wish to combine their initials. These styles are commonly used for gentlemen but are also popular for a modern twist throughout the home. Example: Nicholas Robert Barlow

THREE-LETTER MONOGRAM —TRADITIONAL
The most popular of monogram designs is a three letter format where the surname appears center and larger. Traditional etiquette is to use the lady of the house's initials in the following order: First, Last, Maiden. However, modern tastes have evolved to replace the maiden initial with the husband's first initial.
Example: Eloise Benton Morris, Eloise & Benjamin Morris

TWO-LETTER MONOGRAM —CIPHER
A cipher is a decorative 2-letter monogram that can be used to combine a first and last name (dropping the middle or maiden initial) or two different last names when the partners both keep their last names.
Example: Mary Benton, Lauren Mahoney & Robert Baker

TWO LETTER MONOGRAM —TRADITIONAL
A two-letter monogram in a traditional format will place both letters side by side and the same size, and like the cipher can be used to either combine a first and last name or to combine two last names. Example: Meghan Patterson, Samantha Matheson & John Palmer

MATTRESS SIZES

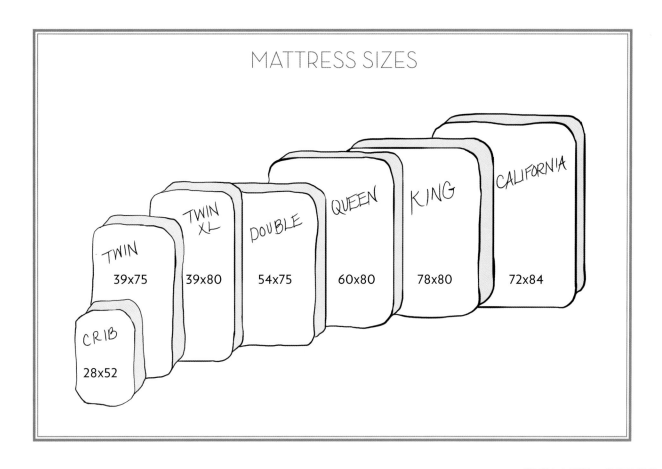

TWIN 39x75

TWIN XL 39x80

DOUBLE 54x75

QUEEN 60x80

KING 78x80

CALIFORNIA 72x84

CRIB 28x52

PILLOW SIZES

26x26 EURO

20x36 KING

20x30 QUEEN

20x26 STANDARD

12x16 BOUDOIR

20x60 BODY PILLOW

5x16 NECKROLL

TOWEL SIZES

Bath Sheet	36x70
Bath Towel	30x59
Hand Towel	20x30
Fingertip	12x18
Wash Cloth	12x12
Large Mat	26x43
Medium Mat	28x35
Small Mat	15x23

NAPKIN SIZES

Cocktail Square	6x6
Cocktail Napkin	6x8
Tea Napkin	13x13
Lunch Napkin	18x18
Dinner Napkin	20x20
Large Dinner Napkin	22x22
Buffet Napkin	24x24
Banquet Napkin	27x27
Lapkin	22x34

GLOSSARY

APPLIQUÉ   Ornamentation created by sewing fabric in a decorative outline to a base fabric and cutting away the excess to create a design.

BATH MAT   A mat or washable rug used to stand on when entering or leaving a bath.

BATIK   A method of dyeing fabric by which the parts of the fabric not intended to be dyed are covered with a removable wax. The design created is also referred to as "batik."

BATISTE   A fine, plain-woven fabric made from various fibers and used especially for finery.

BLANKET COVER   A decorative covering placed on top of the bed, classically made in a single ply of a woven pique or matelassé. The blanket cover is typically the building block for designing the decorative bedding that adorns the bed. Also known as a bedspread or coverlet.

BLOCK PRINT   The method of creating a printed pattern on fabrics by using carved wooden or metal blocks that are dipped in dye and then stamped onto the fabric.

BODY PILLOW   A long oblong pillow, typically twenty by sixty inches, designed to offer sleep support. The body pillow functions well as a singular decorative element when covered with a French case because it's proportion complements queen and king mattress widths.

BOLSTER   A long, cylindrical pillow or cushion used in furnishings. The bolster can be a nice decorative element when selecting the pillow assortment for a bed, offering a new shape to break the monotony of the traditional rectangular pillows.

BORDER   A decorative design of either appliqué or embroidery that outlines or frames the perimeter of an item, whether it is the top of the mattress, the pocket of a pillow, the foldback of a flat sheet, or the edge of a placemat.

BOUDOIR SHAM   A small decorative oblong pillow (twelve by sixteen inches), also called a baby pillow for its popularity in layette sets. The boudoir pillow is a layering piece when selecting a pillow assortment for the bed.

CHAIN STITCH   See Ring Stitch

CHENILLE   A fabric made with a fringed silken thread of the same name used as the weft in combination with wool or cotton, creating a protruding "pile" or texture. Chenille's origin is French, meaning "silken cord" or, literally, "caterpillar." Chenille is a common casual fabric for a blanket cover.

CIPHER   A monogram style wherein two (and sometimes more) initials are intertwined one on top of the other for a singular decorative design. Ciphers are an excellent option for non-traditional monogram treatments.

CLING   The ability of high-quality down fibers to adhere to one another, creating an even layer and removing large pockets of air for superior insulation. Cling is a property found only in the mature down of a few species of waterfowl.

COCKTAIL NAPKIN   A small napkin used for serving beverages. Available most commonly in a six-inch square or six-by-eight-inch oblong shape, the oblong shape is more traditional and is preferred for monogramming or embellishment.

DAMASK   Damask is a fabric that features woven scenes of floral patterns, intricate geometric designs, or simple scenes of domestic life. It may be woven of silk, wool, linen, cotton, or synthetic fibers. A unique feature of authentic damask is that the fabric is reversible.

DINNER NAPKIN   A square of fabric, typically twenty-two inches or larger, used to protect the diner while at the table. The most popular applied embellishment for a dinner napkin in traditional fine linens is a monogram, placed diagonally in one corner, to be displayed when folded as part of the place setting.

DOBBY A decorative woven effect on either end of a terry towel wherein the typical loop-weave breaks for a patterned jacquard weave. The term dobby refers to the loom attachment that creates the pattern.

DUVET A bed covering that is comprised of two layers of plain-woven fabric that are filled with a batting and then sewn into equal chambers to allow for even distribution of the fill. Down is the recommended fill and requires a cover fabric that is both lightweight and tightly woven. Because both the down and the fabric is expensive, a duvet cover is recommended to protect the duvet from wear and tear.

EMBROIDERY An embellishment created by sewing thread onto a fabric in a decorative pattern. The most common uses of embroidery in fine linens is to add a monogram or decorative border to the item. While machine embroidery is most prevalent today, hand embroidery is highly valued for both its rarity and artistry

FINGERTIP TOWEL A small towel (twelve by eighteen inches) in either linen or terry, traditionally used as a guest towel. The origin of the fingertip towel was as a companion to the finger bowl presented to guests for cleansing at the dinner table.

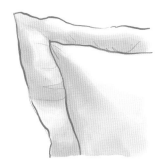

FLANGE An excess panel of fabric that extends from the pocket of either a French case or a duvet cover for decorative effect.

FOLDBACK Also called "the turnback," the foldback is the lead edge of the sheet that is folded over the blanket, exposing the reverse side of the fabric. For that reason, that reverse side is often embellished with a decorative border or a monogram.

FRENCH CASE A decorative pillow cover with finished edges and an envelope style opening on the reverse side. Also called a sham, the French case is typically embellished with a border inset on four sides and/or a monogram placed on the face.

FRENCH KNOT An ornamental stitch made by looping the thread three or four times around the needle before pulling it through the fabric. French knot is a technique that is most typically found on terry towels due to its heavy nature.

FRETWORK A decorative border originally found in metal and woodwork, commonly of a geometric design. Named after the fretsaw that was originally

used to create the cutwork patterns in woodwork, fretwork motifs are now prevalent in all areas of home décor, including linens, and are a universally appealing decorative option.

GREEK KEY A modern term for a meandros pattern—a single line that is shaped into a repetitive pattern. The Greek Key is a classic element of Greek and Roman architecture that is prevalent in all aspects of home décor.

GREIGE All raw textile materials, when they are in natural form, are known as greige goods, meaning that both natural impurities and those byproducts of production are still present in the fabric. No fabric is naturally white and has to be dyed to achieve white. This is the very reason that often times using household bleach will grey linens over time, as the bleach is actually returning the linen to its original greige state.

GUEST TOWEL A small towel in fine linen, recommended for the powder room when hosting guests. Guest towels range in size from that of a fingertip (twelve by eighteen inches) to a larger hand towel size (eighteen by thirty-two inches) and are best suited for the delicate nature of embroidery embellishments.

HAND-GUIDED MACHINE A type of sewing machine that requires hand guidance from an operator. As opposed to modern automated and digitized machinery, a hand-guided machine is designed to work on a single piece at a time and requires full manipulation by an artisan. Hand-guided machines are rarely used today in the manufacture or embellishment of linens and are prized for the quality and durability of the artisan's work.

HANDKERCHIEF A small piece of linen, silk, or other fabric, usually square, used especially for wiping one's nose, eyes, face, etc., or for decorative purposes, such as a men's pocket square.

HEIRLOOM A family possession handed down from generation to generation. In gardening terms (and in terms of fine linens), it refers to an old variety that is once again being cultivated.

HEMSTITCH An old technique wherein threads are drawn out from the hem and the cross threads are stitched together to form a pattern of openwork. Today the technique is often mimicked by piercing the material with a large machine needle and then stitching around the perforations.

HOSPITAL CORNER A fold on a bed sheet or blanket made by tucking the foot or head of the sheet straight under the mattress with the ends protruding and then making a diagonal fold at the side corner of the sheet and tucking this under to produce a triangular corner.

HUCK   Short for huckaback, the term for a woven style of linen originating in Ireland. In Europe huck towels commonly replace terry for all sizes; however, in the United States the huck towels are generally limited to guest towel sizes.

JACQUARD   Named for the jacquard loom that produces it, jacquard is a general term for a variety of fabrics including brocade, damask, and matelaisse.

LAPKIN   A special type of dinner napkin of oblong shape, designed to cover the lap. Most commonly vintage or antique and of European origin, lapkins are typically in a heavy damask style of linen and often have a white embroidered monogram centered on the panel.

LINENSENSE   A fact or tip about fine linens that makes selecting, using, decorating, and caring for them accessible to everyone.

LUNCH NAPKIN   A napkin that is slightly smaller than the traditional dinner napkin, commonly eighteen-inches square, specifically designed for a luncheon setting.

MONOGRAM   A design of one or more letters, usually the initials of a name, used to decorate or identify an object. Originates from the Greek word *monogrammon*, meaning "a character formed of several letters in one design."

NECK ROLL   A small bolster pillow (approximately five inches in diameter by sixteen inches long) used to decorate the bed.

OVER PILLOW LENGTH   A style of blanket cover where there is enough added length to cover the sleeping pillows.

PERCALE   A tightly-woven, medium weight fabric that has no gloss or sheen. Percale defines the type of weave and not the fabric content itself; however, today percale is most commonly associated with the fine cotton fabrics used for sheeting.

PINTUCK   A small tuck or pleat that is sewn in place, often in multiple rows. Pintucks are a common decoration in both household linens and clothing.

PIQUE   A tightly woven fabric that utilizes a dobby on the loom to create a textured pattern. Common pique patterns include birdseye (small diamond), waffle (small square), and wale (lines). Pique is a highly durable fabric that is ideal for decorative bedding.

PRINT   A fabric where ink has been stamped or pressed to create a decorative pattern.

QUILT   A bed covering comprised of batting—typically cotton, polyester, or wool—sandwiched between two fabrics and then stitched or tufted together to hold the layers in place. While its function is to provide warmth, there are many techniques that allow for decoration as much as utility, including patchwork, trapunto, and white-on-white.

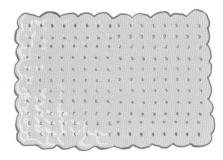

REVERSE SHAM   See Reverse Tuck

REVERSE TUCK   A type of blanket cover that features an additional panel of fabric seamed at the head of the bed, which wraps around the sleeping pillows from underneath, creating a finished look. The lead edge can be tucked in at the front of the pillow, or left to lay flat, and often has a decorative edge for that purpose. Also called a Reverse Sham.

RING STITCH   A style of embroidery stitch where the thread is looped to create a chain-like effect. Ring stitch is special because it is not widely available, particularly with digitized machinery. Also called chain stitch.

SATEEN   A fine cotton fabric woven to achieve a satin-like finish. The origin of the word is a play on the "velveteen," which is a cotton fabric woven with a velvet-like finish.

SEED STITCH   A decorative stitch style that resembles tiny seeds. Seed stitching is almost exclusively found in hand embroidery and is a very intricate detail.

SEERSUCKER   a thin, puckered fabric, commonly striped or checkered, often used for its lightweight and breathable nature. Seersucker is woven in such a way that some threads bunch together, giving the fabric a wrinkled appearance in places. This feature causes the fabric to be mostly held away from the skin when worn, facilitating heat dissipation and air circulation. Its origin is Hindi, as the fabric was created in India during the British Colonial period for expatriates who needed cool clothing to adjust to the extreme heat.

SELVEDGE   The edge of woven fabric finished so as to prevent unraveling, often in a narrow tape effect, different from the body of the fabric. While with bedding and table linens the selvedge is typically cut from the widegood and replaced by a sewn hem, terry towels are commonly woven at their finished width and maintain the selvedge as the finished edge.

SHADING   A decorative technique in embroidery where a second thread color is applied to one side of a design to create a shadow effect. Shading is extremely rare in digitized embroidery and is best accomplished by handwork or hand-guided machine.

SHAM   See French Case

SLEEPING PILLOW   A pillow on which the head rests during sleep. Covered most often with a pillowcase in a sheeting fabric, the fill of the sleeping pillow should be a very high quality to ensure a comfortable night's sleep. Natural fibers such as down is recommended.

SUZANI   A type of embroidered textile specific to central Asian cultures. Derived from the word *Suzan*, meaning "needle" in Persian, Suzanis are typically a cotton or silk base embroidered with silk thread. The oldest Suzanis are from the eighteenth century and originated as the dowry that the bride would present to the groom on their wedding day.

SWISS FILL   An embroidery stitch style that is filled to create a very raised, smooth affect. Unlike satin stitch or Swiss flat, which can be replicated by digital machine, Swiss fill is unique to hand and hand-guided embroidery techniques.

SWISS TRIM   An intricately embroidered trim, often incorporating lacework, cutwork, and openwork, that is most notably produced in Switzerland. Swiss trim is commonly applied to fine household linens and clothing.

TABLESCAPE   A play on the word landscape, tablescape refers to the decorative elements that make up the dining table for a get-together or event.

THREAD COUNT   The number of threads (both warp and weft) in a square inch of fabric. Thread count is used almost exclusively in reference to sheeting, but is only one metric in determining the quality of the fabric. Equally—if not more—important are the fiber quality and type, yarn size, and finishing technique. The best guide to determining the true quality of a sheeting product is to disregard the thread count number and to instead make sure the fabric is a natural fiber and to feel it on your skin for weight and softness.

TONE-ON-TONE   The use of subtle shade variation when embellishing linens with either applique or embroidery.

TRAPUNTO   A specialized style of quilting that results in a highly embossed effect by outlining the pattern with single stitches and then filling the interior of the stitches with yarn or cotton. Eleanor Beard popularized the technique at her Kentucky studio after discovering the style on a trip to Italy.

TROUSSEAU   Of French origin, from the word *trousse*, meaning "bundle," the trousseau is the traditional collection of household linens that a young woman either sews or collects for use in her married life.

WEDGE PILLOW   A very firm pillow with a prism-shape used to support a person in a semi-upright position. Because of its unique shape, the wedge pillow is a nice layering piece when selecting a pillow assortment for the bed's decoration.

WHITE-ON-WHITE   A style of quilting wherein batting is layered between two singular pieces of fabric and then quilted together in a decorative pattern. The term is used to differentiate the style from that of the more traditional pieced or patchwork quilts of America.

WHERE TO BUY FINE LINENS

CUSTOM & BESPOKE FINE LINENS:

Leontine Linens
3806 Magazine Street, Suite 3
New Orleans, LA 70115
504-899-7833
www.leontinelinens.com

Léron
979 Third Avenue, Suite 1521
New York, NY 10022
212-753-6700
www.leron.com

Matouk
www.matouk.com

Sharyn Blond Linens
2718 West 53rd Street
Fairway, KS 66205
913-362-4420
www.sharynblondlinens.com

FINE LINEN SHOPS:

D. Porthault
470 Park Avenue
New York, NY 10022
212-688-1660
www.dporthaultparis.com

E. Braun & Company NYC
484 Park Avenue
New York, NY 10022
212-838-0650
www.ebraunandco.com

Gerbrend Creations
202 Nieman Avenue
Melbourne, FL 32901
321-952-1551
www.gerbrendcreations.com

John Robshaw Textiles
www.johnrobshaw.com

Kim Seybert
www.kimseybert.com

Leta Austin Foster Boutique
64 Via Mizner
Palm Beach, FL 33480
561-655-7367
www.letaaustinfosterboutique.com

Pomegranate
www.pomegranateinc.com

Pratesi
829 Madison Ave
New York, NY 10021
212-288-2315
ue.pratesi.com

Roberta Roller Rabbit
1019 Lexington Ave
New York, NY 10021
212-772-7200
www.robertafreymann.com

Sferra Bros.
www.sferra.com

FOR ANTIQUE AND VINTAGE LINENS & TEXTILES:

Marche aux Puces
30 Avenue Gabriel Peri
Saint Ouen, France 93400
33 (0)1 40 11 77 36
www.marcheauxpuces-saintouen.com

Susan Simon
646-418-8439
www.susansimondesign.com

Wirthmore Antiques
3727 Magazine Street
New Orleans, LA 70115
504-269-0660
www.wirthmoreantiques.com

FOR CUSTOM UPHOLSTERED LINEN CLOSETS, ARMOIRES AND DIVIDERS:

The Finished Seam
3611 South Atlanta Place
Tulsa, OK 74105
918-633-6940

PHOTO CREDITS

Edward Addeo: 32, 51, 92, 111, 115, 161

Michael Arnaud: 106

Joseph Rey Au: 11, 17, 22 (top, center right, and bottom images), 31, 33, 40, 42–49, 152, 155 (center, bottom left and bottom right), 159 (bottom image), 162–163, 174–177, 184–185, 194–206, 208, 210, 219, 229

Mali Azima, courtesy Elizabeth Elsey: 80

Beth Webb Interiors: 104, 116, 136

Grey Crawford: 103

Roger Davies: 102, 111, 131, 142

Down Décor: 225

Erica George Dines: 94

Pieter Estersohn: 76, 140

Pieter Estersohn, courtesy of Architectural Digest: 154

Scott Frances / Otto (Interior Design by Mark Hampton LLC): 24–25, 68

Trey Freeze, courtesy Leigh Taylor Bornitz: 151

Tria Giovan: 130

Matthew Hranek: 120

T. Jeanson: 98–99

Stephen Karlisch: 110

Reed Krakoff, courtesy Pamplemousse Design: 109, 145

Francesco Lagnese, courtesy Veranda Magazine: 103

Richard Keith Langham: 123, 126–127

Brian J. McCarthy: 12

William Meppem, courtesy Martha Stewart Weddings: 57

Charlotte Moss: 11, 224–225

Victoria Pearson: 78

Eric Piasecki / Otto: 36 (Interior Design by David Kleinberg Design Associates, courtesy Architectural Digest); 124, 125, 139 (Interior Design by Katie Ridder Inc.); 132, 156 (Interior Design by Larry Laslo)

Jose Picayo: 122

Eric Roth, courtesy Liz Caan Interiors: 90, 144

Heather Schmidt: 23 (right), 41

Sferra Fine Linens, LLC: 186

Toni Soluri, courtesy Interior Architecture & Design by Suzanne Lovell Inc: 96

Eric Striffler, courtesy Charlotte Moss: 8, 160

Lee Thomas, courtesy Matthew Carter Interiors: 95

Megan Thompson, courtesy MMR Interiors: 128–129, 146, 158

Trevor Trondo, courtesy Frances Schultz: 90

Johnny Valiant: 118

Stacey Van Berkel: 38

Miguel Flores Vianna: 207

ACKNOWLEDGEMENTS

I HAVE BEEN BLESSED throughout my life to know the most engaging, vibrant, and clever people; they have shaped me both personally and professionally, and have illuminated my path often unbeknownst to me at the time. This book is simply another milestone in a very charmed journey, for which I thank everyone who greeted and guided me along the way.

To everyone who has ever placed an order, however large or small, since the launch of my business from a wonderful shotgun cottage on Leontine Street, thank you.

To the hands that have lovingly cut, sewn, quilted, stitched and pressed a Leontine product and to the support team that through the years has helped me create a bridge from artisan to client: Thank you sincerely for your devotion that helped launch a small folly into an upscale provider of fine linens to many special homes and people since 1995. To Nancy Mingus, the ladies of Eleanor Beard Studio, and Fatima Vaz for letting me learn from the masters how to carry on such a treasured legacy.

All my love and thanks to my immediate family, who has sacrificed and supported me the most. To Philip, who saw the vision first and understood what Leontine Linens could become. Philip and I share our first "baby" Leontine Linens and then the other two came right along. To Talley and Nalty, who have slept under the love of a Leontine "berbersh" many nights when mommy was on the road building the business and was not there in the flesh—thank you for being you and for loving me!

To Mom, Dad and Joy—thank you for instilling in me not only the appreciation of those things that came before us but also the work ethic to cultivate them once again.

A special thank you for helping me raise all three babies goes to Kirstin Izzard Keiser. Without you what would we be?! I am so proud to have you at my side and in my life.

I have nothing but infinite gratitude to the friends, advisors and designers that believed in me and in Leontine. Special thanks to Brian Bockman, Chesie Breen, Gerrie Bremermann, Helen Nalty Butcher, Gwen Driscoll, Vesta DeYampert Fort, Judy Goodman, Alexa Hampton, Gigi Lancaster, Keith Langham, Charlotte Moss, King Offutt, Angele Parlange, Laura Vinroot Poole, Melissa Rufty, and Deb Shriver.

Many thanks to those in the editorial world who shined a light on Leontine Linens and gave us a national stage for our philosophy and our wares; especially Kathryn Brookshire Brown, Kevin Sharkey, Martha Stewart, and Newell Turner.

This book itself was its own birth. Thank you to Rizzoli for believing I could turn out an updated and relevant book on living with linens. Special thanks to my editor Ali Power for her expertise and council every step of the way and to Phil Kovacevich for his beautiful design. I owe immense gratitude to Fritz Westenberger, Gwen Driscoll, Tracy Bross, Allan Kukral and Kirstin Keiser for their discerning eye and ear toward both the styling and the written word of the book. Thank you to Inslee Haynes for her divine illustrations. And to Paul Costello and Joseph Rey Au, thank you for your keen sense of beauty in the photography of the book.

To everyone who contributed their most lustrous pearls of wisdom that fill this book: Mark Badgley, Gwen Driscoll, Alexa Hampton, Cathy Kincaid Hudson, David Kleinberg, Keith Langham, Amanda Lindroth, Suzanne Lovell, Elizabeth Mayhew, Mary McDonald, Darcy Miller, James Mischka, Amanda Nisbet, Alex Papachristidis, Laura Vinroot Poole, Suzanne Rheinstein, Katie Ridder, Melissa Rufty, Frances Schultz, Nathan Turner, Beth Webb, and Gay Wirth.

To those designers and photographers whose incredible talent is displayed through the photographs of these pages: designers Margaret Bosbyshell, Leigh Taylor Bornitz, Gerrie Bremermann, Liz Caan, Matthew Carter, Eric Cohler, Elizabeth Elsey, Suzanne Kasler, Delphine Krakoff, Larry Laslo, Brian J. McCarthy, Andrew Raquet, Walker Simmons, Ruthie Sommers, and Rob Southern; photographers Edward Addeo, Roger Davies, Pieter Estersohn, David Halliday, Eric Piasecki and Megan Thompson to name a few.

To Charlotte Moss, for her mentoring and for believing in me with such gusto. Without her assertion that the world needed this book, it would not have happened.

First published in the United States of America in 2014
by Rizzoli International Publications, Inc.
300 Park Avenue South
New York, NY 10010
www.rizzoliusa.com

2015 2016 2017 / 10 9 8 7 6 5 4 3

Printed in China

ISBN: 978-0-8478-4216-2

Library of Congress Catalog Control Number: 2013953944

Editor: Allison Power
Design: Phil Kovacevich
Design Coordinator: Kayleigh Jankowski

Frontispiece: Intricately embroidered monograms on fine silk and linen.

Pages 4–5: Custom appliqué borders in shades of lavender and dusty pink
stacked in an armoire.

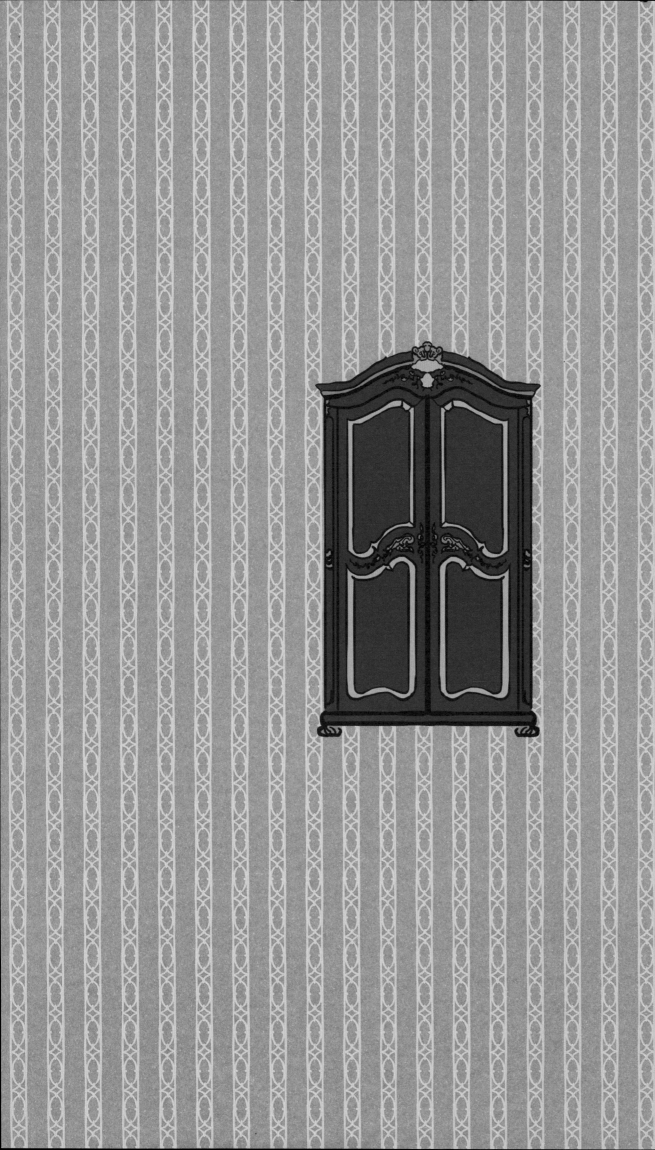